SPECIMEN HUNTING

A GUIDE TO CATCHING BIGGER FISH

First published in Great Britain in 1993
by Boxtree Limited

1 3 5 7 9 10 8 6 4 2

Edited by Helen Douglas Cooper
Designed by Anita Ruddell

Colour origination in Hong Kong by Rainbow Graphics
Printed and bound in Great Britain by Bath Press Colour Books

Boxtree Limited
Broadwall House
21 Broadwall
London SE1 9PL

A CIP catalogue entry for this book is available from the British Library.

ISBN 1 85283 444 7

SPECIMEN HUNTING

A GUIDE TO CATCHING BIGGER FISH

Edited by Neil Pope
with a foreword by Len Arbery

B☙XTREE

CONTENTS

ACKNOWLEDGEMENTS

The editor and publishers would
like to thank the following:

Malcolm Lane for use of his illustrations.

Bob Atkins and Angus Murray
for use of their photographs.

Thanks also to all of the anglers, especially Len Arbery, Bob
James, Matt Hayes, Lee Jackson and Mick Brown, who have
helped contribute to *Improve Your Coarse Fishing* magazine
since its launch in 1991.

FOREWORD

Just why the pursuit of specimen fish has provided me, and countless other anglers, with so much pleasure is difficult to explain, especially to the uninitiated. All I know is that ever since experiencing the thrill of that first quivering roach, extracted from Barnes Pond on a makeshift rod and line not long after World War II, I have been a hunter of big fish. Each succeeding season has witnessed the birth of new aims and objectives. Initially, any fish over 1 lb in weight would suffice, no matter what the species. Then particular species were targeted: perch, roach, pike, chub, barbel, tench and, finally, the mighty carp, in that order. This, in turn, led to the quest for bigger specimens; and, more than 40 years after the capture of that first roach, the enthusiasm still remains. However, there is more to it than that.

My search for big fish has led me around some of the most delightful, exciting and exclusive waters in England. Redmire Pool: the home of giant carp and haunt of all those famous names of the past like Dick Walker, Peter Thomas, Fred J. Taylor, Maurice Ingham, anglers who illuminated the path for the rest of us to follow. The Royalty Fishery on the Hampshire Avon: this was where F. W. K. Wallis and the Hon. A. D. Tryon caught their record-equalling barbel, not to mention the record chub caught respectively by F. W. Smith, G. F. Smith, and Bill Warren, the doyen of this country's barbel anglers in the 1950s and 60s. Throop Fishery on the Dorset Stour: still the home of some of the most impressive river fish. The pits of the Colne Valley, Longfield, where I saw the biggest common carp of my life; Savay, where, perhaps, the next record carp will come from; Wraysbury, where Phil Gooriah extracted the current record tench; the Long Life pits, the River Kennet, the Longford syndicate waters on the upper Hampshire Avon...the list goes on.

Big-fish angling has also brought me some of the finest friends a fellow could wish for, anglers like Bob Buteux and Bill Quinlan, two of the finest fishermen of my generation. Then there is Ron Chant, without whose help my 14 lb barbel would not have been landed; Kevin Clifford, who first encouraged me to write of my fishing experiences; Jack Hilton and the late Tom Mintram, who allowed me to join the Redmire syndicate in 1973; fellow Carp Catchers' Club members like 'BB', Fred J. Taylor and Maurice Ingham, all of whom have indulged my passion for angling memorabilia, as have angling legend Peter Stone, and Chris Sandford, Bob James, Chris Yates and Hugh Miles, the stars and makers of the best angling series yet filmed A Passion for Angling; and, finally, Peter Drennan without whose help and trust these words would never have been penned.

If the pursuit of specimen fish brings you only half the blessings it has brought me, you will still be very fortunate indeed. So enjoy this book, learn about the tactics needed for success, and then go out and catch that big fish. It won't be easy, but with a little patience and persistence eventually it will happen.

Best wishes to you all,

Len Arbery.
Captor of a 14 lb barbel and winner of the Drennan Cup in 1990.

Anglers dream about roach like this superb fish from the Hampshire Avon.

THE JOYS OF SPECIMEN HUNTING

The stillness of the lake is broken by ripples emerging from the thick bed of lilies. It is a welcome sight because the only obvious signs of life on this sultry summer morning have come from chattering swallows skimming the still-misty surface.

A fat mirror carp tries to steal the limelight as it rises in the middle of the lake and then crashes back into oblivion.

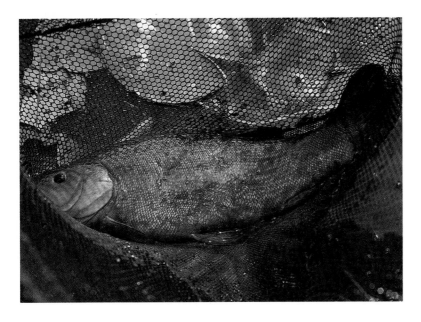

A tench in the net. There can be no greater delight for the summer angler.

9

However, this day belongs to the tench, the angler's early-season favourite. Not to be outdone by that glory-seeking carp, a pair of tench cruises among the lilies, brushing against the stems and making the whole plant shudder.

A bead of light shines through a gap in the pads and catches the backs of the two fish. It jolts them into action as if they have been scared by the sudden glint of sunlight. The larger of the two tench – the female – has an air of grace about her as the paddle-shaped tail propels her plump body forward. Her partner – a sleek male fish with distinctive rounded fins – looks on. He seems to live in awe of the female and is quite content to bask just under the surface and feel the warmth of the bright sunshine.

Their dark shapes, camouflaged in the thick weed growth, display an air of authority that is noted by other aquatic life. Perhaps it is the sharpness of their deep red eyes that make others keep their distance. No living creature can question the beauty of these tench – they must be the ultimate prize for a summer angler.

As dusk approaches, another angler's many hours by the riverside are about to pay dividends. Having patiently fed the swim during this warm afternoon and evening he now waits for that all-important first bite. As the sun descends behind a big willow tree, surface activity on the swiftly moving river reveals the presence of a shoal of good-sized roach feeding on the insect life. An encouraging sign for the angler, but he will choose to wait for one of the bigger fish to accept his breadflake offering.

The angler hopes this preoccupation with the evening hatch will soon be frustrated and that the roach will then turn their attentions to other tasty morsels. Much of his mashed bread feed will have been washed away by the current, but he hopes that some will have remained in the swim, and that the big roach, with hunger in their gills, will now make it their source of food.

Sitting some 30 yd upstream of the feeding shoal, he carefully casts his Avon float into their path and through deft control of his centre-pin reel he is able to present the bait perfectly. Surely his moment of glory will come. In successive casts he lands fish of 8 oz and 10 oz, but he knows bigger fish lie below. However, they are not as easily fooled as their younger cousins.

On the next cast the bait makes it through to the bottom of the 4-ft glide and a scale-perfect 2-pounder leaves the sanctuary of the weed-bed. Temptation has proved too much to resist. The float dives under, and after a spirited battle the angler's patience is rewarded when a brassy flank surfaces to reveal his prize. A dream is realised as the fish of a lifetime sparkles in the waxing moonlight.

These two stories illustrate the attraction of fishing for specimens, but they also show that this branch of the sport allows the angler to appreciate the beauty of the countryside around him. This must not be forgotten by anyone just starting out on the road to becoming a specimen hunter. Too many of today's big-fish anglers are blinkered in their thinking that a 30 lb carp or a 10 lb barbel are all that matters. Often they are disappointed and soon give up the sport for another pastime.

Any kind of fishing should be enjoyed to the full, and specimen hunting is no exception. If you set out with the intention of getting as much out of the countryside as you do out of your fishing, you will enjoy the sport even more. You will begin to read things that are happening above and below the surface of the water, and as a result you will become a better angler, catching more and bigger fish into the bargain.

Specimen hunting is a strange term because it is difficult to determine what is a specimen fish. For an angler used to catching 6 oz roach, a fish of 1 lb could be regarded as a specimen. It is all relative to the venue you fish and to your ability. This fact is important to remember because you must not set yourself impossible goals. If you do, you will become disillusioned. Start off sensibly, and gradually climb the ladder to the point where you are ready to target the really big fish.

This book is an aid towards achieving your goals. Its aim is to show how individual species should be approached and the ways to catch them. Hopefully, by the end of the book you will feel confident about hunting for the bigger fish in your rivers and lakes. It may also help you to choose which species to concentrate on. You may prefer to be an all-rounder, fishing for tench and carp in the summer and for roach and chub in the winter; or you may want to concentrate on one species, like pike. Whatever way you turn, enjoy your sport, and make the most of our beautiful countryside.

CHAPTER ONE

STARTING OUT

What constitutes a big fish? The chub is not a massive specimen but many anglers would regard it as big.

The most important qualities that a good specialist angler should develop are basic angling skills and watercraft. The successful specimen hunter will have served an angling apprenticeship; for instance, he will know how to read a swim, trot a float and leger effectively. Since specialist angling is based on a process of elimination, the newcomer to this branch of the sport should already be familiar with catching average fish plus the occasional specimen, and the wider his

12

experience the better.

Big-fish angling is all about being selective. While the pleasure angler is happy just to catch fish of any size, the specialist isolates a particular species and a target weight. Having done this, he must select the water or waters that he thinks will produce the right results, eliminating those that fail to meet his expectations. The same process must be applied to baits, tactics, weather and water conditions, and swims. Trial and error is the key, because this will ultimately develop into experience, enabling the angler to make short cuts and find the winning combination more quickly.

There are other important qualities needed by the specialist and these relate largely to the angler's temperament.

You will need to use specialist gear for most big fish.

Perseverance, rather than patience, is a virtue. The angler's brain should always be working, and the best specimen hunter is able to get inside the mind of his quarry. This ability comes with experience. It may seem a little alien to you at the moment, but by continually trying to anticipate what the fish will do next, you will gradually become more proficient at predicting its behaviour. There is no question that intuition plays a part in the catching of big fish, and fortune will always

13

favour the angler who is prepared to take a few risks now and again. At the end of the day, specialist anglers need conviction and dedication to sustain them through inevitable blank sessions.

Specimen fish

What exactly is a specimen fish? Well, everything is relative to the water and the angler. On some rivers a 3 lb chub is a specimen fish, while on others it is nothing unusual. You should not be swayed by the hype you read in the angling weekly publications because you could easily set yourself goals that are not achievable. Set yourself realistic targets; it is pointless fishing for a 4 lb chub if you have never caught a 3-pounder, and even more so if the river you are fishing does not hold them.

It is a fact of life that some rivers and lakes hold larger specimens than others. In some Midlands lakes a 20 lb carp is a top fish, while in some of the southern pits a 40-pounder is an achievable target for the most dedicated anglers. Unless you are prepared to travel hundreds of miles in search of a 3 lb roach, it is better to attempt to catch 1 lb and 2 lb fish from your local stretch of water. Progress stage by stage from a 3 lb chub to a 4 lb fish and then a 5-pounder is much more satisfying than trying to hit the high spots immediately. Today, a 3 lb chub might be your target, while in 10 years' time you may be directing your attentions at a 5 lb fish. Remember, though, that you should never stop enjoying catching lesser fish. If you do, give up the sport and take up golf or snooker.

Getting started

Being shown the ropes by an experienced specialist angler is a luxury that few get the opportunity to enjoy. Having gained a grounding in basic angling the first piece of advice is to select your target species. To maximise your chances of success, try to select a species that you have a reasonable chance of catching close to your home, and fish at the time of year that will maximise your chances. In summer and autumn it is best to fish for barbel, carp, tench, bream or rudd, while in winter, pike, chub, roach, perch and dace make ideal targets. After deciding on your target species, you must then make certain that your tackle is adequate for the job in hand. Expert advice in the tackle shops is a good bet, but you must select equipment that gives you the optimum chance of landing your quarry. It is pointless to plan the rest of the

14

campaign to perfection, only to lose the fish due to inadequate tackle when you eventually hook it. Remember that big fish are often found in the most difficult swims with plenty of snags, and the tackle should be chosen with this in mind.

Specialist gear does not necessarily have to be expensive. Quality equipment can be bought secondhand from the disillusioned anglers who have not done their homework and have packed up the sport as a result of their lack of success. While it is fair to say that long-stay fishing – four-day sessions on the banks of a lake – requires lots of paraphernalia, short trips do not. You do not need buzzers, bivvies and bedchairs to catch carp. They just make the process more convenient and comfortable, especially if you intend to spend many hours by the side of a stillwater. You will catch lots of fish and you will learn more by stalking fish, floater-fishing and floatfishing particle baits . You will become more aware of what's going on and be forced to interpret fish behaviour. Feel your way into specimen hunting, catch a few fish, and then make the big investment.

The selection of certain species will minimise the investment needed in extra tackle. You will require no extra gear to pursue specimen rather than average roach for example, and you will get better results by varying your tactics, baits and fishing habits. Chub are similar. In fact, the less gear, the better, especially if you have to move swims constantly.

A through-actioned Avon-type rod, a few legers or SSG shot and size 6 to 12 hooks coupled with 3 lb to 8 lb line and a landing net should see a few fish on the bank, while your bait requirements will be satisfied by worms, bread, luncheon meat and cheese. You can work wonders with a loaf of bread. Tench and bream will frequently respond to simple floats and leger tactics just as readily as to sophisticated approaches.

Swim selection

First-hand experience of a particular venue, or even a precise swim, is invaluable. If you know a water that holds your target species, and where the fish are the right size, that is a good starting point. Failing this, tackle shops are a good bet, as are the venue reports and fishery features in publications like *Improve Your Coarse Fishing* and *Angling Times*.

Having been pointed in the right direction, you could visit your chosen water as often as possible. Don't take tackle at this stage; just explore the water quietly and thoroughly, tactfully observing other anglers and looking for signs of fish. If you spot an obviously competent specialist, approach him

15

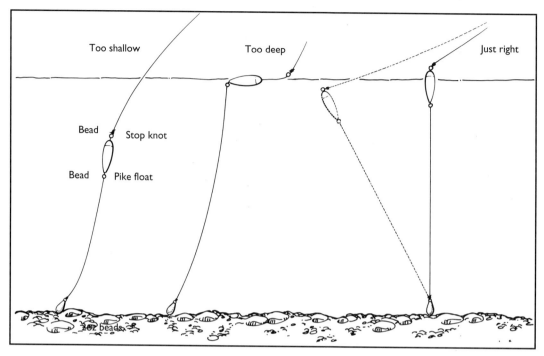

Too shallow

Too deep

Just right

Bead

Stop knot

Bead Pike float

2oz beads

Above: how to find the depth on a river.

Right: what you need to plumb the depth on stillwaters.

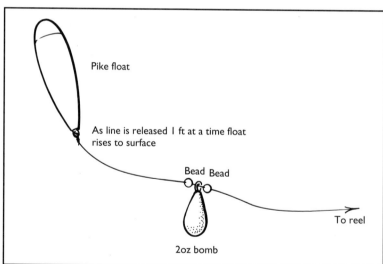

Pike float

As line is released 1 ft at a time float rises to surface

Bead Bead

To reel

2oz bomb

politely and discreetly. Exchange pleasantries before asking a few questions, and it is certainly worthwhile explaining your inexperience and desire to learn. Although you will get rejections, most genuine anglers will be helpful, provided that you don't make a nuisance of yourself. Make sure you don't wear out your welcome.

It is worth investing in a pair of high-quality polarising glasses. These will eliminate glare from the water and open up a whole new world. Remain quiet and take advantage of bankside cover. Soon you will learn to spot fish and the signs

16

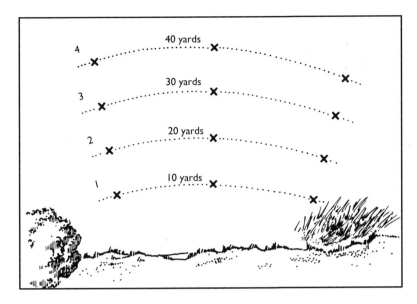

Cast to spot number one, then two and so on. Draw the float back to feel the nature of the bottom.

of fish. Species like carp are fond of basking on the surface and can often be found under bankside foliage or in weed-beds, while pike and perch will betray their presence by striking at fry. On rivers, barbel and chub can be spotted in the shallows while roach, bream and tench love to roll on the surface, particularly at dawn and dusk. Explore the water thoroughly, noting interesting features like weed-beds, overhanging trees or depth changes.

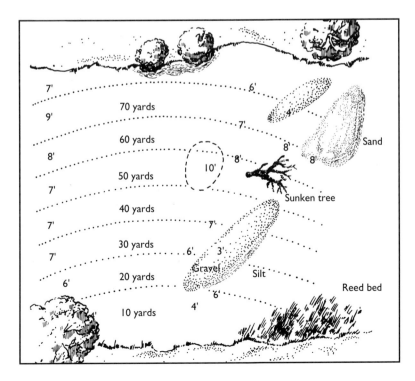

A typical map for a stillwater swim. Draw one of your own on your next trip and then keep it for future reference.

17

Having established the visible signs, the next stage is to carry out further exploration by plumbing the depth. At this point you may have seen a mouth-watering venue and be raring to go, but discovering the contours of the lake or river bottom is worth the extra effort. To avoid the temptation of fishing, take only your plumbing tackle and maybe a compass to the fishery. Begin by drawing the lake on a notepad, marking the directions north, east, south and west. At a later stage you will make good use of this by noting the behaviour of the fish according to the prevailing wind direction. This is also important on a river; it is vital to know that a northerly wind will be a howling downstreamer, for instance.

Start by plumbing all the likely looking areas, marking depth variations and snags or features on the map. The more precise the detail, the better. The plumbing tackle you should use consists of a heavy leger weight (a 2-oz leger is ideal) and a pike float. Make casts progressively further out, marking the depths as you go. Repeat the process to the right and left before moving to the next swim. On a river, plumb the near bank, middle and far bank, repeating the process before moving a few yards downstream.

Establishing the depth is easy. For a lake, cast out the float and tighten down to the bomb, paying out 1 ft of line off the reel at a time. Pause between each release, and count. When the float appears you have found the depth. For instance, if the float appears at a count of six the swim is 6 ft deep. Plumbing the depth on a river is slightly more difficult due to the effects of the current. Fix the pike float by threading the line through the middle, fixing an estimated depth with a stop knot. Six ft is a good starting point. Move the stop knot up and down until the float sits perfectly upright in the water. Too shallow and it will sink; too deep and it will lie flat; just right and it will lock nicely for a few seconds before being forced under by the current.

By adopting this procedure you will establish more than the depth when you retrieve the line. Wind in slowly and you will be able to tell the state of the river bottom. A series of 'jags' on the rod-tip indicates gravel while a smooth retrieve shows up sand or firm silt. A bomb that is hard to free indicates mud or a weed-bed. Check the bomb after the retrieve for signs of weed. A leger that feels as if it has snagged but comes free and plunges away suddenly indicates a gravel bar, while a leger that refuses to come free shows a sunken snag. Having found an underwater feature, establish its extent by a detailed exploration of the area.

Once this vital process is complete, draw the most detailed map you can manage, marking features in the distance and aligning them to landmarks such as unusual trees, church spires and buildings.

Keep a record

By noting the effects of the weather and water conditions on your fishing, you will learn to fish at the most productive times. By co-relating this information to the swims you have fished, you will select the right area. By recording the successful tactics/methods/baits in given conditions, you will arrive at the winning combination more quickly than you would if you fished 'blind'.

It is worth keeping an angling record. As a matter of course, record all the relevant data after a successful or even an unsuccessful session. The key criteria are: swims fished; the time of day; the weather/wind direction; rigs used; baits used; water temperature; weights of fish caught and the time of capture. A picture paints a thousand words and a few simple drawings of the rigs and swims aid recognition.

It is worth consulting your diary frequently to look for trends and patterns, and to study the results gained in the weather conditions you are likely to encounter during the next session. This will help you select the venue likely to produce the best result on the day, and in many cases the species you should go after. You will soon see patterns emerging. For instance, you will probably notice that it is not worth fishing for chub in a fully blown flood, but if the water temperature is high barbel and roach will be prime targets. Equally, it is nice to reflect on previous sessions, reliving former glories, particularly if it is minus 10°C outside and the stillwaters are frozen.

Choice of baits

The range of baits open to the specialist angler is vast, and often it is a case of personal preference. However, some species and venues respond better to certain baits, and it is often a case of finding out what works on your fishery. Some anglers believe that bigger baits will catch bigger fish, but this is not necessarily true. However, large baits do prove to be more selective. Carp anglers, for instance, will use boilies because their hard outer skin will deter nuisance fish. Also, a tiny gudgeon will not be able to engulf a lump of cheese intended for chub, while a big lump of breadflake will attract the larger roach.

Fishing with large baits carries with it a psychological factor. You must have confidence in the bait, and initially this can be particularly difficult for the maggot and caster enthusiast. However, a few bites and several specimen fish on the bank will soon put this right. It is vital to give big baits a fair trial.

19

A scenic stretch of river. It is probably stocked full of good-sized fish.

Night fishing

There is no question that a lot of specimen fish are caught at night, though dawn and dusk tend to be the most productive periods. However, night fishing is not something to be taken lightheartedly by the inexperienced. Apart from the obvious psychological fears of the dark and nocturnal disturbances, there are real dangers if you are not familiar with your surroundings.

Youngsters should only attempt night fishing if they are accompanied by an adult, and any angler contemplating a night session should visit the venue in daylight first. A detailed knowledge of the swim will enable you to position baits more accurately and avoid hazards like falling into inky, black water. Simple things like knowing where the bank finishes and the water starts become important when you are playing a big fish in the dark.

Get yourself organised before the light goes. This means setting up a bivvy and bedchair, laying out a sleeping-bag, siting the gas stove, and arranging tackle in an orderly fashion. Familiarise yourself with the surrounding area. For instance, you need to select a spot where you can land a fish. It is not always possible to do this in the swim you are occupying, so locate another spot nearby. Cast each rod while it is still light, and then tie a short length of monofilament on your main line near the butt ring. This will help you to cast accurately in the dark, because when the monofilament starts

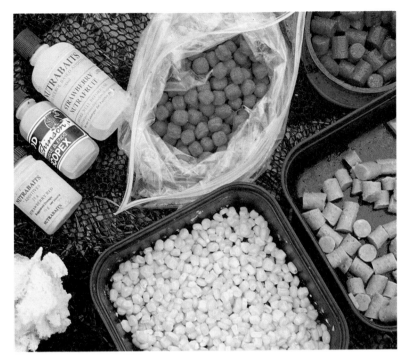

Many baits of all shapes, sizes, flavours and colours are used to catch specimen fish.

to rattle in the rod rings it is time to feather the line. Pick out objects on the far bank that you think will create a visible silhouette in the dark. Trees are the obvious things to choose, and they will help you to cast in the right direction.

Comfort is of paramount importance, so you will need warm clothes and plenty to drink and eat. Take a decent sleeping-bag because it can get quite cool at night, even during the summer months. A gas stove is not a must, but it is useful for making warm cups of tea and coffee. If you haven't got a stove, take a flask with you. You can go without food, but a hot brew will help to keep your body temperature high even on the coldest nights. Two torches – one powerful and the other dim – are also a must. The dim torch should be used for baiting up, tying up new rigs and netting fish. You should aim to shine the beam on the water as little as possible to avoid spooking your quarry. Use the powerful torch only in emergencies and, of course, for finding your way back home or to the car.

If you are frightened of the dark, do not even consider night fishing. There can be many weird sensations for people unused to being alone at night. Some anglers love the atmosphere, others hate it. If you are the least bit uncertain, then don't go. In these circumstances the best advice to give you is to improve your technique. Big fish will feed at some point during the day, and by using watercraft and skill, there is no reason why you should not hook a specimen fish during daylight hours.

CHAPTER TWO

WATERCRAFT

There is much more to fishing than casting a baited hook into the swim. One of the most important aspects of fishing for big fish is watercraft, whereby the angler uses skill gained over a period of time to weigh up a venue. It is certainly not a question of turning up at a venue, picking a swim and bagging up. Watercraft is all about nature, such as discovering how a small stream or river changes quickly from deep, slow-running water to faster shallows. This knowledge will help you to locate your quarry, and find the spots where the fish lie and feed.

Try to remember all those things that happened when you fished as a youngster, because the more information you can store in your mind, the more your understanding of watercraft will develop. For instance, you may recall that when a river or stream was fining down – water running off after a flood – this was one of the best times to catch fish. The extra colour in the water caused by the rainfall seemed to act as cover for the fish and they became more confident about feeding. All the little things you learned as a boy should help you in your adult years, and it is this process that turns you from an average angler into a good one. There are no short cuts, but by watching for certain signs you should pick up fundamental things quickly.

You should not get the impression that watercraft is a complicated subject because it isn't. It's commonsense. Go to a venue and try to read the water. Just by looking at the fishery you will be able to spot the tell-tale signs of fish, and with a little experience you should be able to tell which species are present. For instance, a pond may be clear, with the odd lily-pad and reed-fringed margins – that sort of venue cries tench and rudd. Large gravel pits may look frightening, but if they are heavily coloured it usually means that a good head of bream is present. These pits will also be home to species like roach, tench and perch. Heavily stocked carp waters – good venues for the inexperienced specimen hunter – are easily identified by their excessive colours, caused by the fish stirring up the silty bottom to feed. By using watercraft the angler will be able to recognise fish-holding swims at different times of the year and then remember where he found them.

Signs

To help you to identify more clearly the way the angler needs to spot the places to fish, let us take a stroll along an imaginary stream. There are bound to be similar streams or small rivers in your locality, and they are certainly great places to learn about watercraft.

The first feature you are likely to come across is an overhanging bush on the far bank. There is also deepish water in this swim, and it looks like the ideal spot for chub, who gain confidence in the cover provided by the bush. The approach here would be to feed a little upstream of the bush and run a float down underneath it.

A little further downstream of this bush is a dead branch lying in the stream, creating inviting-looking slack water. In this slack the water is almost stationary compared to the main flow, which is pushing through after a couple of days of rainfall. The beauty of this swim is that fish – chub and roach – will be holed up on the edge of the slack water, moving out occasionally into the main flow to pick up morsels of food before swimming back behind the fallen branch. The next spot is an apron where the deeper water runs into the shallows. This is a great summer holding spot for chub because they like to lie in the extra flow where there is more oxygen in the water. However, they do not enjoy the rough water too much and so stay in this middle area.

Moving up to the shallows you will be able to see fish darting around over the gravel bottom and between the streamer weed. These will be mainly dace, although roach will be mixed in with them. Again they thrive on the high oxygen levels created by the broken water. If it is bites you're seeking, then this is the place to trot your float, but the fish will tend to be on the small side.

Some of the features to look out for when you're on your travels.

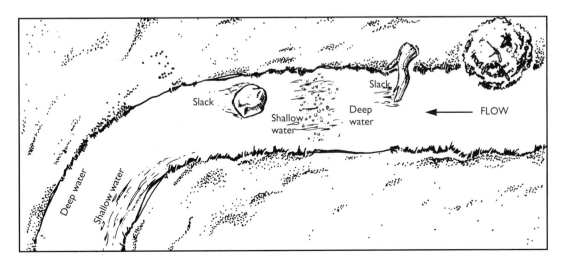

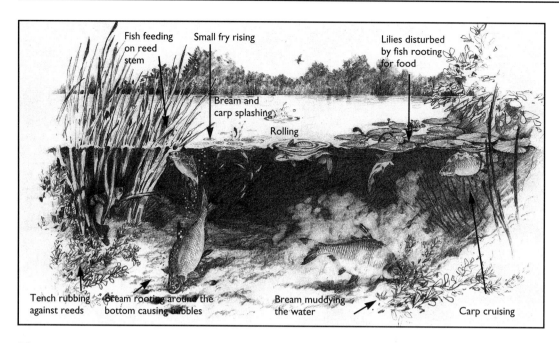

Fish feeding on reed stem

Small fry rising

Lilies disturbed by fish rooting for food

Bream and carp splashing

Rolling

Tench rubbing against reeds

Bream rooting around the bottom causing bubbles

Bream muddying the water

Carp cruising

There are many signs of fish activity . . . here are just a few.

Below the shallows there is a big boulder sticking out of the water. Like the dead branch, this stone creates an area of slack water where, especially in winter, fish can escape from the main flow but still catch food items drifting downriver.

Sooner or later you will reach a bend in the river, and this is normally a superb fish-holding spot. On the inside of the bend there will probably be a silty bank with shallow water, while on the outside, signs of the stream deepening off will be apparent. There will be undercut banks – eroded by the current – on most bends, where chub can hide, only to be tempted out at feeding time. Usually there will be a slower pace near the bottom of the swim, as opposed to a faster one near the surface where dace can be found.

On this particular stream there is a sluice gate, and the pool below the waterfall is another superb fish-holding spot. In fact, it is probably the top area on the stretch, providing a good depth to give the fish cover while it is highly oxygenated because of the falling water.

It is worth remembering that fish habits alter as the seasons change. In summer when the oxygen levels are low, more fish can be found in the shallower water with streamer weed. In the cold winter months the less active fish will go into the deeper, slower bends out of the main flow.

Fish spotting

Location is 90 per cent of specimen hunting, and another method of making sure you are fishing in the right spot is by fish spotting. Too many anglers arrive at a fishery and settle

Above: Keep a low profile when stalking fish.

Left: Polarising glasses are ideal for spotting fish. During the closed-season it is worth taking a few samples of bait with you to see the fish's reaction when they are thrown into the water.

25

down in what they believe are 'fishy'-looking swims. However, after several hours of fishing they are still biteless. The reason: they have not spent enough time finding out where the fish are feeding. One of the best ways of finding the fish is to go on a spying mission, and you may find that spotting fish gives you as much enjoyment as fishing itself.

So when and where do you start? A calm and sunny day provides the best conditions, and it is ideal if the sun is towards your back, rather than in front. If it is directly at your back you could cast a shadow over the water. In these circumstances the need for stealth is paramount, and you must approach the margins of the lake carefully.

There are many good spots from which to study fish activity. Some anglers prefer to climb trees to get a picture of what is going on. When the water is clear, it is possible to sit up a tree all day and see every fish in the vicinity. However, when the water is coloured you have to look for other signs. There is no quick way of interpreting these, but with experience you will soon be able to recognise them with confidence.

There is no point in taking a lot of gear with you. For one thing, you will scare the fish by clambering along the lakeside or riverbank, and for another it is not much fun lugging a lot of kit around. All you really need is a pair of polarising spectacles, binoculars, notepad and pencil. An Ordnance Survey map of the area may also be of great use to you in helping to pinpoint certain features.

If you need to buy polarising glasses get the biggest available,yellow-tinted glasses are generally best for the job in hand. The human eye is more sensitive to yellow light than to greens or blues, and consequently you can see more. When climbing trees it is advisable to wear shoes with a good grip. You will be certainly able to view the water at a better angle, and as reflection off the water is no longer a problem, visibility is improved.

Visible evidence

There are many signs that give the game away. The inexperienced may take some time to recognise them, but after a while they will become second nature. The main signs are bubbles appearing on the surface, rolling fish, coloured water in otherwise clear conditions, and movement of reeds and lilies. There is always a danger when anglers see bubbles on the surface that they mistake them for fish rooting about on the bottom. The key is to differentiate between gas bubbles and fish. One way of determining the difference is to watch the bubbles carefully. If they remain in one spot then it is odds-on that gas is coming off naturally. However, if the source of the bubbles moves slightly then they are certainly caused by fish. Gas bubbles can be set off by the fish themselves, either by rooting in the silt or disturbing weed, so if you are not sure, look for other signs.

At some time or other all coarse fish, apart from eels, roll on the surface. Be on the riverbank at the right time and you can make an assessment on the size, species and quantity of fish present. This is where your notepad and pencil come in handy. Write down what you see so that you can build up a picture of where fish are likely to be found at a given time of the day. Experienced anglers can tell by the way a fish rolls what species it is, but there can be pitfalls in this for the less experienced. For instance, on rivers big bream, roach and barbel will roll while chub and dace tend to splash. However, stillwater bream have a distinctive splash. One second you can hear the fish come out of the water and the next its tail slaps the water. On other occasions they will hardly make a sound. If you know someone who can tell the difference between species instinctively, it could pay you to go along with him if he will let you.

Swirling fish create boils on the surface, not splashes. If the water surface is rippled by wind, the swirl of a fish is often shown by a calm patch. In shallow water, swirls can be caused by carp or other fish burrowing in the silt. That indicates a prime feeding area and should be noted. Foraging fish throw up mud, and often colour up the water for yards around – another hotspot to note.

Reed movement is a sure sign of fish, especially tench. In the summer they can cause whole bunches of reeds to move, especially in the early morning. Fish, especially carp, often feed on individual reed stems and if you watch carefully you should be able to spot them quivering.

If your fishery is continually cloudy – often the case on carp fisheries – it is sometimes difficult to spot the fish, so you must look for other signs such as rolling fish, bubbles, boils and reed movement. If it is a water that contains only carp, you will know that these things are caused by carp and you will quickly be able to build up a picture of the prime feeding spots. Don't fish 'blind' because you could waste hours, even days, if it is a big fishery. If in doubt, seek advice from an angler who fishes the venue regularly, and he will probably be only too pleased to help. Don't expect him to give too much away, but a bit of guidance will go a long way.

Sometimes, jumping up and down on the bank can help you to spot fish because it scares them out of their cover. As long as you do not intend to fish on the same day, it is a method of finding fish. Scaring them into movement is sometimes the only way to spot the top swims. Chub usually

27

Some anglers use binoculars to spot fish activity.

hug the bank, and by walking up and down the riverbank you will often entice them out into the main flow. However, you will need clear conditions to take full advantage of this ploy. Remember also, if there are other anglers around they won't take kindly to you jumping up and down, so make sure you do it when things are quiet and a few days before you intend to fish. In fact, it is probably best reserved for the closed season.

Timing

The final few weeks of the closed season are definitely the best time to spot the behaviour of fish, especially on a carp lake. On any warm day between May and mid-June it is possible to watch carp. They seem less afraid of the angler at this time, as though they somehow know they are safe until the glorious 16 June. This fact alone makes it essential for the really keen carp man to visit his water as often as possible before the season starts.

The dedicated angler will want to know how many carp the fishery holds and the size of the fish present. You should be watching to see which bays the fish favour and which

28

routes they choose to travel along from one part of the fishery to another. All this information is central to carp catching, but there is more. Uncrowded banks encourage the fish to move in very close and you can often have them at your feet. You can see every fin and every scale, and watch everything they do. The most difficult task can be to read the signs of carp activity accurately. The really good carp angler wants to know not just where the carp are, but exactly what they are doing. This can make every scrap of difference during the coming season. It may be worth introducing some bait into different swims because it may help you to find out which fish are feeding, preparing to feed or are just at leisure. You will be able to study a carp's reaction to your proposed baits, deciding whether the free offerings provoke interest and desire or caution and even fear. In short, the body language of a carp is of vital interest to the experienced carp angler, and every single thing you can learn about it you can put to good use in the months to follow.

Fortunately, there are several standard behaviour patterns to watch out for, and these do not differ much from one water to another. When any dog growls it is to be treated with caution, and when any cat purrs you know it is happy. So it is with carp. By reading well-telegraphed signs you can tell exactly what its intentions are at any particular moment. Use the final weeks of the closed season to build up a picture of fish activity.

All is quiet and peaceful at the lakeside. This is the ideal time to go fish-spotting.

CHAPTER THREE

START WITH CARP

If you are thinking of taking up specimen hunting, why not start with carp? A species that has gained in popularity over the past few years, carp will give you a real taste for the big-fish scene. However, as you start out on the road to becoming a carp angler, don't set your sights too high. Remember that carp do not start at 20 lb. Although there are lots of pictures of fish over this size published in the angling press, it would be wrong to believe they are easy to catch.

Start with a water that is heavily stocked with fish running right through the range from real babies of 2 lb to 10 lb. This type of fishery is a good grooming ground. Here you will be able to learn how to play and land fair-sized fish, and get an insight into the different baits and rigs.

Fishing the smaller carp waters will also help you to understand the movements of fish, how they react to wind, temperature changes and, of course, angling pressure. It is no good buying all the fancy gear if you do not know the first thing about the species. The heavily stocked water will give you a good foundation on which to build. Lessons learned at this stage will help you in the future.

Tackling up

Most tackle shops will have a vast array of carp rods from 10 ft to 13 ft, and test curves ranging from 1 ½ lb to 3 ½ lb. It's best to start with an 11-ft or 12-ft rod with a test curve of 2 lb, which will be heavy enough to cast a 2 oz leger a good distance and still be forgiving when it comes to playing a decent carp under the rod-tip.

Big-fish anglers often select rods by test curves, but exactly what does this mean? The test curve is a guide to a rod's power; traditionally it was the weight that had to be suspended from the rod-tip to pull it into a 90-degree arc. Test curves are always given in pounds and fractions of pounds, and specialist big-fish rods usually start at around 1

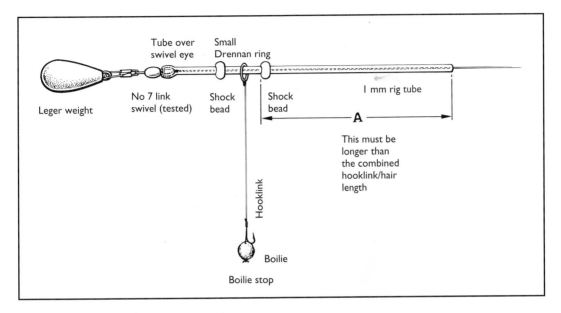

Tube over swivel eye — Small Drennan ring — I mm rig tube — Leger weight — No 7 link swivel (tested) — Shock bead — Shock bead — A — This must be longer than the combined hooklink/hair length — Hooklink — Boilie — Boilie stop

½ lb. You are unlikely to need a rod in the UK with a test curve of more than 2 ½ lb.

Despite all the advances in modern rod technology, the test curve probably remains the safest way of choosing a rod for specimen fishing. As a simple guide, multiply the test curve of a rod by five to give yourself an idea of the best breaking strain of line to use with it. For example, if a rod has a test curve of 2 lb, the ideal line strength will be 10 lb. Of course, it is never quite as simple as that. Cost, material and action as well as length will all be determining factors in your rod choice. Do not feel you have to use a certain breaking strain of line with a rod of a certain test curve. Good rods will handle large fish even if you are not using a line with the 'ideal' breaking strain. Similarly, an experienced hand can use a higher breaking strain line than the ideal one.

Buy a rod with lined rings, especially the butt and tip rings, and a screw-type reel fitting. Big reels tend to work loose on the fittings on match rods. Most modern-day carp rods seem to be fitted with abbreviated duplon handles, which are fine. They may look a little strange compared to a standard match rod, but they are good enough for the job in hand. Some carp anglers will use only black rods with black whippings because of a belief that they will catch more fish with them. That is nonsense. There are many good rods with colourful cosmetic finishes.

Most reels over £20 are of an excellent standard nowadays so you do not have to pay the earth. There are various situations where specialist rods and reels costing a lot of money will be needed, but do not be too adventurous when you are starting out. Buy a reel that will hold at least 150 yd of

The helicopter rig – a superb method for catching carp.

31

This is the moment of truth for the carp angler as he prepares to net his quarry.

10 lb line with a gear ratio of 4:1 or 5:1. Do not get one of those super-fast ratio match reels for playing big carp because they will lose you fish. Some anglers back-wind when playing carp while others prefer to use the clutch. Nowadays, you have a choice of reels, some with the clutch at the front of the spool some with a rear drag. It is wise to find out which suits you before actually paying out your hard-earned cash. Spare spools are cheap to buy so get several. Then you can load them up with 4 lb line (for floatfishing), 6 lb (for open water fishing) and 10 lb to 12 lb (for use in snaggy swims). Use the knowledge you have built up from general coarse fishing to decide the right line strength. It is all very well getting plenty of takes, but it worth nothing if you are broken by a big fish. Make sure you have the right breaking strain for the job.

Choice of hooks is very much a personal decision, but not every pattern in the bigger sizes makes a good carp hook. You may swear by a hook you have been using for maggots but in a size 2 it may be useless for fishing with boilies. Carp have thick rubbery lips so your hookpoint needs to be sharp. The first thing you should do after buying a packet of hooks is to check them with a magnifying glass. Check for a good barb, correctly shaped eye or spade, and sharpness of point. Put the good hooks in an appropriate box and throw the others away. A hook costs pennies, but it could make or break your day's sport.

The angler's pulses are racing as he lands a hard-fighting fish.

The list of accessories is endless. Take a trip to your tackle shop and you will be amazed at the number of carp knives, baiting needles, chairs, bite alarms, stainless-steel buzzer bars and rod-rests on sale. However, be careful, because you can

33

Two methods of making a 'pop-up' bait.

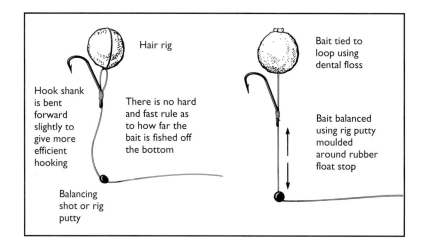

Hair rig

Bait tied to loop using dental floss

Hook shank is bent forward slightly to give more efficient hooking

There is no hard and fast rule as to how far the bait is fished off the bottom

Bait balanced using rig putty moulded around rubber float stop

Balancing shot or rig putty

spend so much money on looking the part that you cannot afford to go fishing. Most important, you will need a landing net with 36-in arms and a strong handle. The pan nets used by match and pleasure anglers are unsuitable both in size and strength. Bite alarms – more commonly called buzzers or optonics – cost anything from £10 to £70 each. You can catch carp without them, but if you expect a long wait between 'runs' they can be invaluable. Even on those small-carp waters, the fish can sometimes take a little time before picking up the bait.

Baits

Do not get carried away with the idea that carp can only be caught on boilies. Maggots, casters, meat, sweetcorn, pastes of various flavours and bread will all take their fair share of carp. However, boilies are the most favoured bait, and many thousands are used by Britain's carp anglers every year in their quest for a specimen fish. The majority of baits used are bought off the shelf, and are so popular because of their convenience.

The top fishermen will most likely use their own baits, prepared in advance at home. They will experiment with mixes, additives and colourings to find a bait that will make the difference between catching a 20-pounder or leaving the lakeside fishless. There is nothing complicated about boilie-making. With a little practice you will be preparing your own baits quickly and efficiently, and the satisfaction you will get from catching fish on them will make the effort worthwhile.

If you have already done some carp fishing you will know that a boilie is a small, round bait. But why is it so called? The simple answer lies in the bait-making process. After being rolled into a small ball, the boilie is placed in boiling water for

34

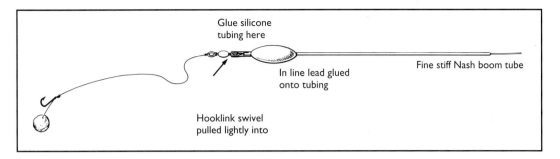

Glue silicone
tubing here

In line lead glued
onto tubing

Fine stiff Nash boom tube

Hooklink swivel
pulled lightly into

a short time to give it a hard outer skin and to help the eggs
in the mix to congeal quickly.

A good anti-tangle rig.

You will find that it is a lot more economical to make your
own baits than to buy shelf-life boilies, and you should
eventually enjoy experimenting with different mixes.
However, do not run before you can walk. Start by using one
of the many boilie base mixes that are commercially
produced in powdered form, and do not go overboard with
exotic flavourings or additives. Ask yor local tackle dealer
which are the most popular brands of mixes because you can
be sure these are very effective.

In the beginning you do not need many tools for boilie
production, but after a time you might like to buy specialist
bait-making systems that will save you time. However, your
wife or girlfriend may not like you using their favourite
mixing bowl or non-stick saucepan, so you may need to
invest in both before you start. A deep mixing bowl is best.

When it comes to ingredients the first thing to buy is your
boilie base mix. Mixes such as bird food or fish food come in
bags of around 4 lb. Many companies sell products for boilie-
making – the majority are excellent – so it is a case of
choosing one of the leading brands. Next, you need eggs. As
a general rule, six per lb of mix is the right amount. In the
beginning flavourings and dyes are optional, but a vegetable
oil like sesame seed oil helps to add essential fats and make
the bait roll out smoother.

Put a saucepan of water on the stove to come to the boil.
Crack three eggs into a mixing bowl. Use a pipette to add
flavouring (if used) to the eggs – 1 ml of flavouring per egg is
the ideal amount. The vegetable oil should also be added at
this stage – 10 ml for three eggs – plus a small sprinkling of
colouring powder. Whisk the flavourings, dye and eggs
together and then add the base mix. You want a sticky texture
so make sure you do not add too much powder or the
mixture will go stiff and be difficult to roll out. Mix the
contents together and then knead into a ball of paste.

Break the paste into smaller balls and roll out with both
hands into sausages. With a knife, chop the sausages into
bait-sized pieces, and then roll each one into a ball between

35

Carp should be handled with care and quickly returned to the water after capture.

both hands. By now the saucepan of water should be boiling. Put about 20 balls in a cooking basket and immerse in the water. Depending on how hard you want them to be, the baits should be left in the boiling water between 30 seconds and 3 minutes. The longer you leave them, the harder they will get. Shake off the water before dropping the baits on to a piece of cardboard to cool.

Rigs

As carp fishing has become more popular in recent years, pressure on fisheries has obviously increased. This has led to greater developments in rigs and terminal tackle as fish have become harder to catch. Consequently, owing to the popularity and effectiveness of ultra-supple hooklink materials, it has now become necessary to use end rigs that help to eliminate any tangles. There is nothing worse than sitting by the side of a lake worrying whether or not your end tackle is tangled. It does your confidence no good at all when you reel in at the end of a night session, only to find that your hooklink is wrapped tightly around your leger weight. It will

36

have been a complete waste of time.

To a certain extent it is possible to eliminate tangles by feathering the line on your cast. This means that you are slowing down the leger weight, and the hooklink is generally held further forward during flight, and as a result enters the water straighter. One disadvantage with feathering the line is that casting distance is cut down. That's no problem if you are fishing at close or medium range, but puts constraints on distance fishing.

For all-round efficiency you will find the best way to eliminate tangles is to incorporate some kind of anti-tangle tubing into your set-up, and this will give the added advantage of protecting your main line from getting roughed up or broken on sharp gravel bars.

There are a number of different permutations on rigs using tubing and all of the ones shown in the diagrams should hold you in good stead. All the necessary bits and pieces to make up these rigs are available from most good tackle shops. For the helicopter-type rigs shown, use 1/2 mm black PVC tubing;

The carp-angler's set-up with two rods waiting and ready for action.

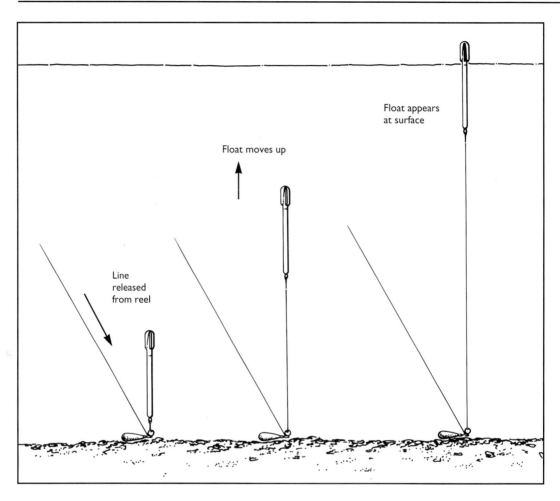

Float appears
at surface

Float moves up

Line
released
from reel

After casting, release line from the reel 12 in at a time until the float appears at the surface.

for the other rigs, fine stiff boom tube is ideal. The stiff tubing will improve your casting distance because it adds extra lift and more stability to the leger weight in flight. As an example, imagine throwing a javelin without its long tail section – it would not go very far.

Having decided which anti-tangle rig to use, you next have to decide how to present your hookbait. The 'in' thing over the past few years has been to use popped-up hookbaits – floating boilies fished anything from 1 inch to 1 ft off the bottom of the lake. Pop-ups are a very effective method because they are clearly visible to the fish and waft about enticingly should a fish swim nearby. Carp, being generally inquisitive creatures, sometimes can't resist sampling them whether they're interested in feeding or not. There are a number of different methods that can be used to make pop-ups. The most common is to cook boilies in a microwave oven for three to four minutes. You can also bake them in an ordinary oven, grill them or simply roll polystyrene inserts into baits before boiling them.

38

A recent innovation that has come about because of the use of pop-ups is the bent hook. When used correctly, the bent hook can lead to extra fish on the bank because the hook turns more easily when a carp ejects the bait and catches inside the mouth. One problem, though, is that bent hooks inflict more damage to the fish's mouth than normal hooks, therefore it is unwise to advocate their use. You should stick with the more normal hooks because if your bait presentation is right you will still catch lots of fish.

Surface fishing

Surface fishing for carp is one of the most enjoyable and successful ways to catch fish, and yet too few anglers take it very seriously. Especially on warm and sunny days, it is worth giving it a try, probably before all other methods. The sight of surface-feeding carp taking floating baits can set the pulses racing as you wait in anticipation for a fish to pick out your hookbait. The beauty of this method is that you don't need much tackle. You can walk around a lake with one made-up rod, a landing net, a bag of bait, and a catapult. It cuts out those long sessions on the bank; in fact it's ideal for those short early morning or evening fishing trips.

It is not necessary to have special rods and reels for surface fishing. However, it is probably better to use a softer-actioned rod because you will sometimes be fishing with lighter breaking strain hooklinks. Therefore, the softer action of the rod will provide a buffer against the sudden lunges of a hard-fighting fish.

The rig should be a fairly simple but effective set-up. Thread your main line – 11 lb would be sufficient – through a bead and then a surface controller float before tying it to a size 10 swivel with a five-turn grinner knot. For surface fishing use a nylon hooklink with the lightest breaking strain you can get away with – 5 lb is about right. However, if you intend fishing a fairly snaggy water then you should use a

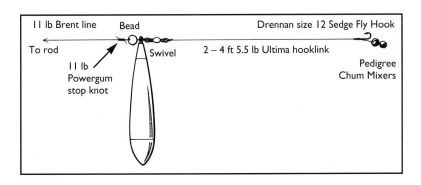

11 lb Brent line   Bead   Drennan size 12 Sedge Fly Hook

To rod

11 lb   Swivel   2 – 4 ft 5.5 lb Ultima hooklink
Powergum
stop knot   Pedigree
                                                   Chum Mixers

A good rig for surface fishing for carp.

39

**Above left:
Many anglers prefer
to roll their own
boilies, using specially-
made machines.**

**Above right:
Boilies have become
the staple diet of carp
in many waters.
A throwing stick is
often used to fire
them out into the
swim.**

stronger line.

A size 12, lightweight and extremely sharp hook should be tied to the hooklink with a knot shown in the diagram, which also forms the hair for your hookbaits. The other end of the line is attached to the swivel mentioned earlier. To complete the rig, tie a Powergum stop knot above the bead, which obviously prevents the controller float from sliding up the line. With the float fixed in position it sometimes helps to prick the fish into bolting.

When it comes to a floating carp bait you can't beat Pedigree Chum Mixers. Drill your hookbait samples with a special drill available from tackle shops before mounting them on the hair rig. Once the hole has been made use a baiting needle to thread the Pedigree Chum Mixer on to the hair. Use two for the hookbait and keep them on the hair with a hair stop.

All you need now is a catapult to fire loose offerings of Chum Mixers into the swim. Initially, spread the feed over a fairly large area, and then wait for at least half-an-hour to allow the carp to build up confidence. When you are about ready to fish, begin to concentrate the feed and this should gradually pull the carp into a smaller area where you intend to fish your hookbait.

It is best to cast beyond the baited area and then draw the tackle back. Casting among the floaters could easily spook the feeding fish. Try to make sure that your hookbait is left at the edge of the floaters because carp usually take these samples first. A pair of good-quality polarising glasses are an essential item for surface fishing because they help to take the glare of the sun off the water as you watch for movements around your controller float.

You can fish a controller float at long range, but it is a far better method at shorter distances of around 30 to 40 yd,

A plump carp in the net. Don't set yourself too high targets because fish like this common carp will give you an exciting battle.

where the top of the float can be seen fairly easily. More often than not, a fish that takes a bait will hook itself with the set-up described. The line between rod-top and float will tighten dramatically, and a scrap with a hard-fighting fish will begin immediately. Try to spot any signs of fish near your controller, and strike at any sudden movement of the float. Usually, you'll soon know when a fish has taken the bait. Always hold the rod because of the violent nature of any takes.

More often than not, you will catch two or three fish quickly and then notice a lull in the action. This is the time to give the swim a rest and allow the fish to gain confidence again. Keep introducing loose offerings and you will soon find the fish back on the feed. However, carp are a very suspicious species and if you start fishing again too soon they will ignore your baited hook.

Plumbing the depth

Finding the depth of your swim is of paramount importance if you want to be successful at catching carp. It's no use just casting out your baits and hoping, yet far too many of today's anglers do just that. You need to find the contours of the swim and any features like gravel bars that aren't visible even if you have the most expensive polarising glasses. Time spent discovering possible fish-holding or fish-patrolling areas will pay handsome dividends later in the session. It only takes a few minutes to find the deeper and shallower areas of your swim.

Use any normal rod, but mark the butt section 12 in from

41

the reel mount. This mark, made with Tipp-Ex, will help you to estimate the depth of the swim. As well as a reel loaded with good-quality line, you will need a float. There are various floats on the market that are ideal for the job although a vaned drift float – used in pike fishing – is preferable. It has a slim, pencil design with vanes on the tip, which certainly helps to cast long distances and is very visible. The slimness of the float makes it very aerodynamic both in flight and also underwater. As you pull it through the water you can feel for features, unlike most bulky floats, which do not give you the same kind of touch. Other bits and pieces required are a 2 oz or 2 ½ oz leger weight, two link clips, a bead and a run ring.

The rig used for depth-finding is simplicity itself. First, attach the link clip to the run-ring before clipping it to your leger weight. Then thread your reel line through the ring and bead before tying it to the other link clip, which is attached to the bottom of the pike float. You will need a leger ring of some sort to allow the float to rise in the water after casting – an ordinary swivel would easily get clogged up with weed and prevent line from running through smoothly.

It is best to cast to the furthermost point, and then keep drawing the tackle back as you find the depth of swims at different distances. After casting out, tighten up the line immediately and sink it. The float and leger weight will now be on the bottom of the lake. Open the bail arm of your reel and feed off line with your left hand until you reach the 12-in mark on your rod. This process is continued until the float appears on the surface. If you have fed line off the reel four times to the required mark you will know the depth of the swim is 4 ft – 12 in multiplied by four equals 48 in. Easy, isn't it? Keep repeating this process until you have a clear picture of your swim – the deeper drop-off areas, gravel bars and other, shallower marks.

Once you have decided at what range you want to fish, it is best to cast out your depth-finding rig, checking once again how much water you will be fishing in. Leave the float in the water because it is a good marker for your loose offerings of bait. Using your catapult or throwing stick, you can feed with great accuracy around the float. Then cast your actual fishing tackle to the marker before retrieving the float. You will be certain of the depth of water and also that your hookbait is near your loose offerings.

Finding features

What do you do after finding the depth of your swim? Good question, and one which often confuses a vast number of anglers. It has to be borne in mind that a lake is like a fish's

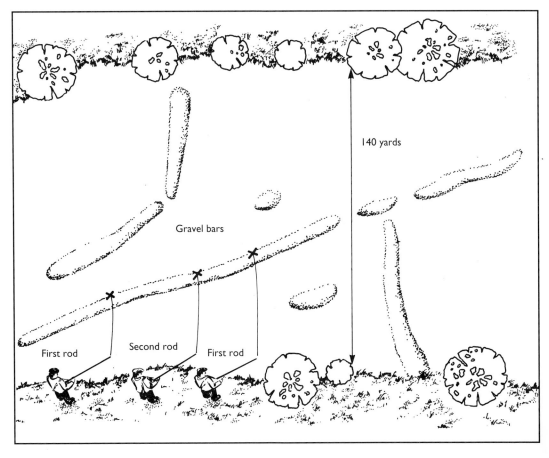

140 yards

Gravel bars

First rod

Second rod

First rod

Here's how to find gravel bars in a water. Note the leapfrogging effect of the two rods to find the direction of the bar.

house. There are areas for playing, areas for sleeping and areas for feeding The latter is obviously the place you are most interested in finding. For instance, a slight deviation in the lake bed may signal the dining-room table. However, you may be able to create a feeding spot by groundbaiting with a few free offerings of the chosen bait in and around the area.

Bear in mind your reason for choosing a particular swim. If you have seen some evidence of fish, you may spook them by casting around with a plumbing rod and firing out free offerings of bait. In this case, a softly, softly approach is needed; tackle up as quietly as you can and then cast out your tackle with as little disturbance as possible. Then sit back and see what happens. Prior knowledge of a few swims will be invaluable in situations like this. It is very worth while forfeiting a day's fishing for a day's plumbing. One day's fishing is a small price if it pays dividends in the future.

A walk round the lake on a hot sunny day - when the fishing probably wouldn't be any good anyway - with a bottle of cold drink to quench the thirst, a plumbing rod, a few spare leads, some floats and a notebook, will prove invaluable in future. Note down all you find and keep it for

43

future reference. Despite the fact you won't actually catch anything, you should really enjoy your day out.

So what are you looking for? It's all very well knowing that one particular area is 1 ft deeper than the surrounding water, but what relevance will this have? When feature finding, the angler should be trying to form a picture of the lake bed. This has to be done by not only finding depths but also 'feeling' the lake bed - something you get better at the more you do it.

After casting out, keep your plumbing rod fairly low, almost parallel to the water. Slowly drag your leger weight along the lake bed by bringing the rod round by your side, at the same time watching the tip. If the area is silty, you will feel a fair bit of resistance on the rod-tip as the leger is obviously sinking into the silt. If this resistance then disappears, it could be that you have pulled over an area where the bottom is made of a firmer material such as clay or sand. It is preferable to fish on these areas as your hookbait and free offerings will be more visible and accessible to the fish. If you feel a series of short taps on the rod-tip, you are probably pulling the weight over a clean, gravelly patch. This is another favoured area because it is usually kept clean by the regular attentions of feeding fish. On the other hand, if the tip locks up and it suddenly becomes fairly difficult to pull your leger along, then this could be because you have pulled up against a gravel bar. This can be confirmed by letting your marker float up to the surface, at the same time measuring the depth. Reel it back down again, drawing in your leger weight a fraction, then checking the depth again. If it is a gravel bar, obviously you will get shallower readings until your leger drops off the nearside of the bar.

Fishing on the slopes or tops of gravel bars can be very productive as the fish use them as roadways to swim around the lake. As these bars are often covered with mussels and snails they can be productive natural feeding areas. You may need to make quite a lot of casts around the same area to confirm your findings. In order to find the direction a bar follows, it is preferable to have another rod set up in the same manner – with the same weight of leger and same type of float.

Once you have cast the first marker float onto the bar and it has popped up to the surface, cast the second rod out to either the right or left of the first but further out. Draw back the tackle on this rod until you feel the bar again, at which time let the float rise to the surface. Once you have noted the second float's position, you can retrieve the first rod and cast back out to either the right or left of the second float. By following this leap-frog procedure with the two rods, you can fairly quickly determine the direction of the bar. Obviously, at the point where you cannot feel the bar, it has either ended or there is a gap in it. If you cannot feel it with your second cast it, could be because it runs directly away from you; either that, or it is not a bar at all but a gravel hump or plateau.

Setting up

Having done your homework on a few swims - plumbing the depth and feature finding - the next task is to set up your tackle. Ideally, you should make up your rods at home and carry them to the water in a rod holdall. The main advantage of carrying your rods ready made-up is that it will save a little time when you get to your swim, and you can start fishing a little quicker. This can be very beneficial because sometimes you do catch within a few minutes of casting out, especially in high summer when the most productive period is often first thing in the morning. And in winter, when temperatures around the lake are hovering around freezing point, your tackle will be much easier to set up in the warmth of your living-room.

One thing you should do before casting your tackle into the water is to roughly set the clutch on your reel so that it gives line should your rod be pulled down past its test curve by a powerful carp on its first run. Often, when a run occurs, it comes out of the blue and can take you by surprise. If the fish takes off at a rapid rate, and you are not prepared, you can often lose the fish either because your line breaks or, what is more common, because your hook pulls out of the fish. To set the clutch, thread the line through the rings of

How to tie a hair rig.
Step 1: Tie a loop in one end of your hooklink. Thread the other end through the back of the eye of the hook, leaving enough line between the eye and the loop to form the hair.
Step 2: Bring the end of the line round into a loop and thread the end through the back of the eye again.
Step 3: Take hold of the line, forming the large loop just in front of the hook eye and make four turns around the shank, moving towards the bend of the hook.
Step 4: Holding the turns in place, moisten the knot and pull on the other end of the hook length to tighten.

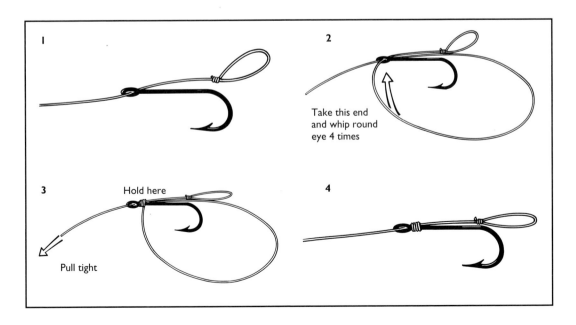

1

2

Take this end and whip round eye 4 times

3   Hold here

Pull tight

4

your rod, and pull the tip down by way of the line until it arcs round to its approximate test curve. Keep loosening the clutch until it just starts to give line. Don't pull the rod-tip round at too sharp an angle because this might compress the material, causing it to snap.

You are now ready to cast out. Usually, you have the rods pointing in the direction that you intend to cast. Although this is not absolutely necessary it just means that in doing so your bite detection system – monkey climbers – will work more efficiently.

After casting out, it is entirely up to you whether you fish with your line tight or slack from the rod-tip to leger. On some of the more intensively fished waters carp have become wary of tight lines, therefore it may be preferable to fish with them slack. There is one disadvantage with this, however, which is that you will not spot 'drop-back' bites very easily. Drop-backs come about when you are using a fixed leger rig. With conventional running-leger set-ups there is no problem, because in whatever direction the fish moves after picking up the bait, you will get a registration on your indicators. If, however, you are using fixed legers and a fish picks up the bait and moves towards you, this will only usually register if you are fishing with fairly tight lines in conjunction with heavy monkey climbers.

There are many different types of monkey climber available, but the principle behind all of them is the same and involves a nylon or PTFE body that slides up and down a stainless-steel needle. It is preferable to fish all types of monkey climbers in conjunction with bite alarms because then you have an audible as well as a visual indication of a bite. As a result, you can sit back and relax once the baits are cast out and scan the water for signs of fish, read a book or whatever.

The most popular type of bite alarm is the optonic. This involves a wheel, a paddle plus a clever bit of circuitry, all nicely packaged together into what looks like a little black box. Once cast out, the rod is placed on the rod-rests, and the line rests on the wheel of the optonic. Any movement of the line, whether forwards or backwards, turns the wheel, which is attached to a paddle that runs between a light circuit inside the alarm. Every time the paddle breaks the light beam, it causes a beep. Obviously, the faster the wheel turns, the faster the beeps, hence the saying 'a screamer'.

Your reel has to be set so that it can give line should a fast run occur, otherwise your rod could be pulled into the water, even by a relatively small carp. Some anglers set the rod on the rod-rests with the bail arm open so that a running fish is free to take line. Others have their reels set in order that they can turn the handle backwards, bringing about more sayings like 'reel spinners' or 'churners'. Nowadays, however, a better system is available to the carp angler by way of a baitrunner system.

With a baitrunner-type reel you disengage the spool of the reel by way of a lever found on the top and back of the reel. The reel is able to give line on a run without any fuss or the possibility of any tangles. Then, with a slight turn of the handle, the baitrunner facility is engaged, leaving you to play your fish.

Ideally, you should put your chair close to your rods so that you can strike a bite easily from a seated position. Knowing when to strike should a bite occur will come with experience. If, as is often the case with modern-day rigs, it is a real screamer, then it will be obvious. Usually the fish is hooked before you even pick up the rod, and as a result all you need to do is lift the rod out of the rest and bend into the fish. A violent swiping strike could result in your snapping your line on the strike.

If you are getting a series of short lifts on the monkey climbers, these could be either bites from finicky fish or line bites. The thing to do, if you are fishing with slack lines, is to watch your line where it enters the water. If it flicks forward quickly and then back, forget it. If it flicks forward and then holds, it might be worth striking. If you are fishing with tight lines, watch your rod-tip. If it nods, then stops quickly, don't bother. If it continues to nod, however slightly, strike. It could be that a fish is already hooked.

Once a fish is hooked, try to keep your cool. Take your time and apply steady pressure. This is a moment to enjoy, and provided your tackle is sound and you don't make any mistakes, the fish should be yours. If you play it properly using adequate tackle and don't make any mistakes, but lose it through the hook pulling out, don't be too disappointed. The moment to savour, however, is when you pull the fish over the waiting net. The anxiety ends, your heartbeat slows and you've achieved what you set out to do – catch a carp.

CHAPTER FOUR

TIME FOR TENCH

The start of any new season is often regarded as a time when tench really come on to feed, providing the angler with spectacular, rod-bending sport during the first few weeks. It is no wonder they have become a firm favourite with anglers because as well as having a silky, attractive appearance, which just makes you want to stand back and admire, they can put up a really good fight.

Once you have enticed them into the swim, you can have a red-letter day with bulging nets of fish. However, it is not simply a case of turning up at the lakeside, choosing a swim, casting out a baited hook and 'bagging up'. Specialist tench anglers will spend two days preparing for a day's sport.

The tench is a delightful fish to catch, especially in the summer.

Clearing a swim

The first job for any good tench angler is to clear out weed from a chosen swim. During the closed season, reeds will have sprung up in the margins, while thick weed will be covering much of the lake bed. Preparation of the swim for tench fishing takes a little time and effort, but it will be worthwhile in the end.

There is no doubt that a visit to your chosen lake a few days before your planned fishing trip is beneficial. Look for signs of tench, especially the movement of reeds and lilies, and then choose a swim you believe will produce fish in a couple of days' time. After three months of closed-season inactivity, your proposed spot will probably be thick with weed that will have to be cut back to make fishing possible.

In order to make the weed-cutting effective, it is best to clear a small patch close in, because then you will be certain that your hookbait will be presented accurately before the fish. If you rake out a patch of weed a good distance from the bank you could not be certain of placing your bait in the correct spot every cast.

The most important item of equipment is some kind of weed-clearing device. You will find it pays dividends to lay your hands on a properly constructed weed rake or drag, rather than using any old piece of iron. If you don't use the proper equipment, you will not manage to clear the swim effectively, and most of the weed will be left in the spot you are trying to clear.

An ideal rake consists of two pieces of metal bolted together in a T-shape with about a dozen metal prongs inserted and welded into the horizontal piece. A fairly long length of strong nylon rope – about 60 ft – is attached to the arm of the rake. The rope needs to be strong enough to retrieve the rake should it happen to catch a heavy snag. Heavier rope might be expensive, but there is no point in taking the time to make an effective rake and then losing it on the first chuck.

Before you start to clear the weed, you may need to cut down a few reeds in the margins. Do not remove all the reeds in the swim, just enough to create a channel for fishing, so you can cast easily and land a fish without it getting snagged up. The removal of all the reeds would ruin the swim. Tench like some sort of cover, and if there are no lily-pads on the lake the reeds will offer sanctuary.

Use garden shears to cut down the reed stalks and any other obstacles that will hinder your fishing. However, it should not be a wholesale slaughter of the bankside vegetation because the angler needs cover as well. Anyway, you would soon incur the wrath of the fishery owner if you

49

removed all living plants. There is not much finesse needed in throwing out a rake and then retrieving it. However, a heavy piece of iron attached to a soggy rope is a difficult thing to throw out at the best of times so it will pay to wade out as far as you can. First, make sure the lake is not too deep or silty. Coil up the rope and with an underarm action propel the rake out into the swim. If the area is particularly weedy, pull the weed out in small steps, gradually throwing the rake further and further out until all the intended area is clear. You should be aiming to make a hole in the weed into which you will drop your hookbait, and then slightly clear a larger patch in the vicinity. This needs to be done to prevent a fish from bolting into dense weed after being hooked. By clearing a channel, a hooked tench can be guided confidently into open water.

After half-a-dozen throws you should start to rake in small quantities of swan mussels along with particles of mud. This is evidence of the weed being cleared and the rake finding the bottom silt. In the interests of conservation, any live swan mussels should be thrown back, although it may be worth keeping a small quantity because they do make a good early-season bait. Once you have raked the reed out of the swim, don't just leave it lying on the bank. Collect it all up, find a bush overhanging the water, and neatly lay the weed underneath it where it will quickly decompose.

Prebaiting the swim

Once you have raked the swim, you need to prebait it. Initially, you want to draw the tench into the area, and the best attractor is hempseed. Throw in or catapult about 4 pt of hemp into the swim and then leave it. The weed raking will also help to draw in the tench because it stirs up the natural food from the silt below.

At this early stage you should not be worried about introducing hookbait samples like sweetcorn. For one thing, sweetcorn is more expensive than hempseed, and for another it has a nasty habit of going sour on the lake-bed if left uneaten. It is far better to introduce a few hookbait samples on your next prebaiting session the following evening.

On your second visit to the lake – the eve of your fishing session – you must drag the swim again because there might still be some weed on the bottom. Loosefeed another batch of hempseed with a few grains of sweetcorn and some chopped-up worms.

The day you have been waiting for finally arrives – the day when you will see if all your hard work and preparation pays off with a good net of fish. Your first task is to lightly rake the swim for a final time. This may seem a little strange, but the disturbance will again stir the tench into feeding as the rake exposes the natural food. Throw in half-a-dozen handfuls of hemp, and a small quantity of sweetcorn. Now give the tench time to settle on to the feed while you tackle up.

Tackle

In the majority of swims in which you are likely to find tench, there may not be much room to manoeuvre, especially if overhanging bushes or trees enclose the spot, so a fairly short rod may be needed. An ideal choice will be an 11 ft 6 in rod with a test curve of 1¼ lb. It may seem a rather powerful piece of equipment for tench, but it will be ideal for playing fish under the rod-tip, especially in snaggy swims. An open-faced reel filled with 4 lb line and a 2 lb to 3 lb hooklength are a good combination when floatfishing, although you may have to use stronger line if carp are present in the fishery. Heavier tackle will give you the insurance against hooking a carp, and at least you will stand a chance of landing it. Finer line will probably mean more bites, but if your raking and prebaiting have worked then there should be more than enough action to keep you happy. A small balsa float is a good choice, and all you will need to lock it into place are two No. 1 shot, with another No. 1 3 in from a size 10 hook. This single shot will be resting on the lake bed so that the hookbait can be fished hard on the bottom.

Bait

There is no doubt that over the years sweetcorn has caught more tench than any other bait. It is best to start your fishing session with a single grain on your hook to judge the response of the swim. If tench have settled on to your loose-fed offerings and prebaited area, a bite should occur soon after you cast out for the first time. However, if you notice a few indications on the float but none develop into a positive bite, it could mean that the tench are a little suspicious of the bright yellow sweetcorn. In this case it may be worth dying some sweetcorn red, using a special dye purchased from your tackle dealer. If the bites still remain tentative the best policy is to try another bait, and the next-best thing is a lobworm from your garden lawn. Choose a fairly small worm, break it into two and hook one piece; the whole worm would be too large for tench. You can also break a few worms into smaller pieces for loose-feeding into the swim.

It is certainly wise to take a selection of baits with you

51

The angler wins another battle with a tench. It has made all that hard work preparing the swim worthwhile.

when fishing for tench, experimenting with them until you find the best one on the day.

If you try a selection of baits and yet the fish still tend to be finicky, it will pay you to change to a different floatfishing method. Another good early-season technique is the 'lift method' where the float is again set overdepth. Use a straight waggler float attached to the line bottom-end only with a piece of silicone rubber tubing, not locking shots. All the float's loading should be fixed 4 in from the hook. When the tench sucks up the bait and rights itself, it dislodges the shot resting on the bottom. The float will start to lift and may even lie flat on the surface. This is the time to strike.

Legering

As well as floatfishing for tench, it may be necessary to try legering a bait, especially on large gravel pits where the larger

Above: Using a rake, pull weed out of the swim in small amounts.

Left: After the swim has been cleared of weed it is time to prebait the swim. Hempseed is a cheap and effective way of drawing fish into the area.

specimens are usually found. The swingtip – a piece of fibre-glass or carbon that hangs down from the rod-tip with the reel line threaded through a tip ring – is a good means of spotting bites when legering. A bite is shown by the swingtip moving towards the horizontal from its original vertical position.

The advantage of a swingtip as opposed to other bite detection methods is that it gives the angler the indication of a

53

bite in the right place – at the front end of the rod. This causes less resistance through the rod rings than other indicators such as a butt indicator. It may pay you to have a secondary indication from optonics, which, used in conjunction with baitrunner-type reels, will allow the line to run off smoothly should a good-quality fish take the bait.

The swingtip, being at the front end of the rod, also allows the angler to see what is happening in the swim in front of him. When tench fishing it is important to spot things like moving lily-pads or reeds, and bubbles rising to the surface, so you can read and react to what is happening.

With the low angle of the swingtip to the water, the angler knows that the line is tight to the leger weight, and as a result the chances of noticing bites are greater, and of missing them, less. If he was floatfishing or legering with the line hanging down from a conventional tip, the angle would be greater and consequently there would be more line to pick up on the strike, increasing the chances of missed bites.

There is no doubt that you will lose ultimate casting distance and marginal accuracy when swingtipping, but this is more than made up for by the convenience of the method. Because the swingtip hangs down from the end of the rod there is a chance that the line will get wrapped around it, so the cast has to be very smooth. Many anglers new to the method get into tangles and quickly give up again, but all that is needed is a smooth swing of the rod. It is important, however, that your reel spool is filled to the correct level: to within $\frac{1}{16}$ in of the lip. If this is the case, the actual cast will be that much smoother.

Once you have cast and the leger hits the water, drop a finger on to the reel spool to prevent any more line from being released. As a result, the leger weight will sink straight to the bottom on a tight line. You must make sure that all of the line sinks as quickly as possible, so treat it with washing-up liquid. Pour some concentrated liquid on to a damp sponge, cast out, and then hold the sponge tight against the line as you wind it in. This will make the line sink more easily. Some anglers have special containers into which they drop the whole spool of line together with the washing-up liquid, and this has the same effect.

Once the line is sunk, place your rod in two rests and tighten up the line even more until the swingtip just about touches the surface. It only has to move $\frac{1}{4}$ in to signal a bite. Obviously, in windy conditions it is not easy to 'rest' the tip on the surface because the skim will keep knocking it about, and it may have to be sunk slightly with the angler looking for much more positive indications. Contrary to the belief that the swingtip angler points his rod directly at the point where his leger has landed, it is better to fish at an angle. Bites are easier to spot this way because the tip is moving across your line of vision rather than away from it.

You can buy special swingtip rods, but it is quite easy to convert a 12 ft big-fish rod. Simply remove the original tip ring and slide a piece of silicone tubing over the end of the swingtip and rod end. This allows the swingtip to hang at the required angle to suit conditions simply by tightening up the line to the right tension. Some anglers prefer to fit a special tip ring that allows a swingtip to be screwed into it. Baitrunner-type reels are a good choice for this type of fishing because they allow line to peel off without the fish feeling resistance.

Keep your leger rig as simple as possible. Use a leger weight just large enough so that you can reach the required distance when casting, and place it on a short link. You can buy link-legers – a leger attached to a short piece of plastic – nowadays and these are ideal. Thread the link-leger and a bead on to the main line, which should then be tied to a swivel. The bead acts as a buffer between the link-leger and the swivel, thus protecting the knot. The other eye of the swivel is for attaching a hooklength.

The hooklength should be around 18 in long, but if bites are not forthcoming you can try to make things happen by varying its length. If you retrieve your tackle and you have not seen any indication that the bait is damaged or missing, you will need to shorten the hooklink to help you to spot bites. If, on the other hand, the bites are little twitches, you should lengthen the hooklink to lessen the resistance. You may find you have to experiment because tench are more sensitive to resistance than most other species. Work between the extremes of as little as 2 in and as much as 3 ft.

Be accurate

Feeding accuracy is vitally important when legering for tench. When fishing a larger expanse of water and casting greater distances it may be necessary to put out some kind of marker. One way is to use a pike controller float, which you cast out on a second rod and anchor on the bottom with a leger weight. For the furthest distances, you may have to row out and drop an empty lemonade bottle attached to a brick with a length of rope over the side of the boat. The length of the rope should obviously equal the depth of water. This kind of marker is ideal when night fishing because it can be picked out easily with a torch. Remember, though, to retrieve the marker after fishing because fisheries will not take kindly to lots of lemonade bottles littering their water.

Even though you will be fishing the leger, it is important to

55

Always take a selection of baits when you go tench fishing. These should include worms, dyed sweetcorn, hempseed and bread.

When night fishing with a leger for tench, the best way of spotting bites is through a starlight attached to the quivertip.

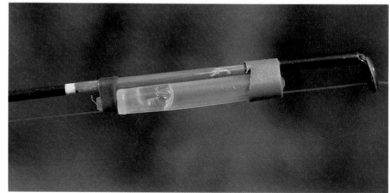

find out the depth and contours of the swim. Do this by casting out the leger and counting how long it takes to reach the bottom. On larger gravel pits it may be necessary to go out in a boat and test the level by dropping the leger over the side. Knowledge of the contours of the bottom can help you to decide where to place your baits. Some anglers like to fish for tench during the hours of darkness so prior knowledge of the swim is of vital importance. When swingtipping in the dark, you need some kind of illuminating device to help you spot bites. The easiest method is to use a starlight – a short piece of tube which, once broken or crushed, glows in the dark for hours on end. Place two pieces of small silicone rubber over the end of the swingtip and these will hold the starlight in place. It can be a really exciting sight to see the starlight on the swingtip move in the darkness, showing a fish taking the bait.

CHAPTER FIVE

FISHING FOR BARBEL

Barbel fishing is not necessarily a sport for hardened specimen hunters. True, the biggest fish will be caught by anglers willing to work hard and spend many hours on the riverbank but there are plenty of smaller barbel in the country's rivers to give the newcomer to specialist angling a fair crack of the whip. If you are new to barbel fishing you will probably want to know the best places. After all, it is pointless going to a river that may have all the qualities of a barbel hotspot and yet does not hold any fish.

The unmistakeable head of a barbel with its distinctive whiskers.

A simple leger rig for barbel.

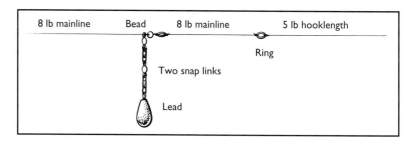

8 lb mainline	Bead	8 lb mainline	5 lb hooklength

Ring

Two snap links

Lead

One way of finding out about the top rivers is to follow the reports in the weekly angling press. These can help to determine the right stretch of river, but, most likely, you will have to visit the venue to decide on exact swims. When you find the barbel, the next priority is to avoid frightening them: don't wear bright clothing; don't make any unnecessary noise or disturbance; keep a reasonable distance from the fish; keep a low profile and don't make any sudden movements. Choose the right time to fish – generally, the first and last two hours of daylight are the most productive.

To give you some idea of where to fish, here is a list of the better barbel rivers: Bristol Avon, Hampshire Avon, Warwickshire Avon, Cherwell, Middlesex Colne, Derbyshire Derwent, Yorkshire Derwent, Dove, Kennet and its backwater Holy Brook, Lea, Loddon, Medway, Mole, Nidd, Great Ouse, Yorkshire Ouse, Severn, Swale, Teme, Thames and its tributary St Patrick's Stream, Trent, Ure, Wensum, Wey, Wharfe, Windrush and Wye. Excellent barbel fishing is controlled by the following clubs: Birmingham AA, Christchurch AC, Leisure Sport AC, London AA, Reading DAA and Ringwood AC. Among the best day-ticket venues are the Royalty fishery on the Hampshire Avon, Throop Fishery on the Dorset Stour and Aldermaston Mill on the Kennet.

Swim choice

When deciding on a swim to fish, look for a steady flow, a clean gravel bottom, and some cover for the fish like a boulder or sunken log. In summer barbel swims are not too difficult to find because, with polarising sunglasses, the fish can be seen in clear water. Barbel also leap clear of the water, and a leaping barbel may disclose the whereabouts of a shoal. The location of swims where the fish can't actually be seen, through 'reading the water', is a more intriguing business, and few anglers seem really skilled in this refined facet of river fishing. This is perfectly understandable because you are dealing with a constantly changing medium and it requires a certain understanding of the make-up and condition of the water – temperature, speed of flow, opacity, oxygen content and 101 other things that combine to make up barbel swims. Barbel prefer deeper, hence slower, moving water and this betrays its presence by giving clues, either singly or collectively, to the observant angler. Here are some of the more usual ones: a smooth, silky surface; a generally darker area of water; where the current slows; where the river narrows, especially if the current shows slight or no increase in speed. A naturally steeper bank often denotes that deeper water exists at its base as well.

Most barbel anglers like to roam about, so don't overload yourself with tackle. Everything should be carried in a rod holdall, rucksack and bait bag because then if you are not successful in one particular swim, you can quickly move to the next without too much hassle. There is so much enjoyment to be gained by keeping on the move, catching one or two fish before switching to a new spot.

The best advice for any newcomer is to find a river that holds a good head of barbel and then take a roving approach, moving from swim to swim until you locate fish. In some places, especially the shallow reaches, you can spot and stalk fish. The larger barbel are found in the deeper, slower runs.

Starting tactics

The choice of whether to floatfish or leger is determined by conditions and situations. For example, you would find it

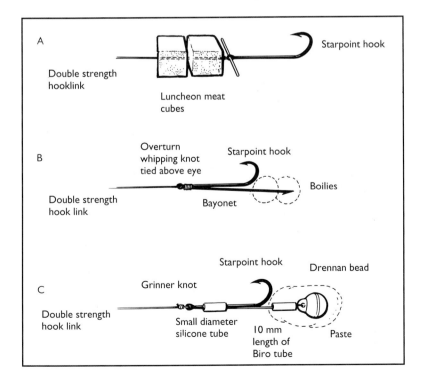

A: Cubes of luncheon meat fished above the hook and kept in position by a small diameter piece of plastic or grass through eye of hook.

B: Drennan boilie bayonet trapped under knot. Used for mounting hard baits such as midi-boilies and cubes of cheese.

C: Hair rig for paste baits. The Biro tube prevents air cutting through the paste, and the bead stops paste coming off easily.

59

difficult to fish a small hole in a weed-bed with float tackle. On the other hand, the current may enable you to guide a float into an area that is inaccessible by any other method. Line strength must be carefully chosen whatever your preferred fishing method – you may be able to go down to 4 lb line when long trotting a clear swim, but you may have to resort to 10 lb or 12 lb breaking strains when fishing adjacent to tough weed-beds and snags.

Although most of the big barbel are taken on leger tackle it is often wise to search out a swim with float tackle first. You will need a specialist rod for trotting a float for barbel, and there is no better way to tackle a moving river than with a centre-pin reel. If you are fishing for average-sized barbel, use 5 lb line on the reel. Your stick float should be made out of balsa. If the swim is fairly shallow and the water turbulent then your shotting pattern should be as follows: with the float attached top and bottom, place 2AAA under it to give stability, and then a bulk of 3BB 18 in from the hook to get the bait down quickly. A No. 4 dropper shot 12 in below the bulk completes the rig.

With double caster on a size 18 strong hook you should now be ready to tackle the swim. If there is a fairly fast flow, loose-feed a handful or two of hemp and a dozen casters slightly upstream, and then you can be certain they will float down through the swim. Do this every cast in an attempt to stimulate the barbel into feeding.

By searching the swim with a float, you should find out if there are any barbel in the vicinity. If you do get bites, it may be wise to change to legering tactics, especially if the larger specimens start to make an appearance. However, if the floatfishing fails to get a reaction, it is probably best to move to a different swim.

Legering

Often a straight leger rig can be more effective than a float. For this type of fishing you will need an 11 ft quivertip rod with a 1 ¼ lb test curve, combined with an open-faced reel filled with 8 lb line. It is worthwhile using a trace or hooklength of 5 lb or 6 lb line. When legering it is important to avoid unnecessary tangles, especially after casting, because you do not want your hookbait lying in a tangled web on the river bed for minutes on end. One way of avoiding tangles is to attach a ¾ oz leger weight to a snap link with a swivel that is clipped to another snap link. The use of two snap links should help to stop tangles forming. The top link is then threaded on to the main line along with a bead, which in turn is stopped by a special ring. Between this and a second ring

tie a 6-in length of 8 lb line before attaching the hooklength. The reason for the short length of line is that it gives the rig added protection should the leger weight wrap itself around the line.

Although undoubtedly preferable, specialist tackle is not absolutely essential, and remember that tackle that suits one situation or individual may not suit another. What is vitally important when fishing for hard-fighting fish like barbel is the choice of lines and hooks. These must be strong and 100 per cent reliable. A No. 6 specimen hook tied to 6 lb breaking strain line would be an average choice, but if in any doubt err

Barbel are one of the most powerful fish in our rivers and will battle hard before finally surrendering to the angler's pressure.

61

on the stronger side. You can always scale down, but you can't undo the damage once a barbel is lost.

When legering, hold the rod at all times. Too many bites are missed by anglers who place their rods in rests. By holding the rod you can react quickly to every bite.

After casting out and allowing the leger to settle, hook the line near the reel around one or two fingers. You can feel for any tightening or pressure on the line caused by a bite, as well as watching for tell-tale signs at the tip. Using this sight and feel approach, you should be confident of hitting most bites. Barbel bites on a quivertip rod are usually signalled by a couple of knocks on the tip before it sweeps round into a sharp curve.

Baits

The barbel angler has a wide choice of baits at his disposal. Maggots, casters, sweetcorn, bread, worms, cheese, luncheon meat, sausage paste, hempseed and midi-boilies are all excellent baits for using in rivers. Rarely will anything else be required. Barbel will readily eat all of these baits, although if you want to avoid the attentions of roach and dace, you may have to steer clear of maggots, casters, sweetcorn and bread. Boilies can sometimes provide a measure of immunity from the unwanted attentions of nuisance fish.

Legering requires the use of bigger baits, and one favourite is luncheon meat. For the bigger specimens you will need to cut the meat into large cubes, although some anglers experiment with irregular shapes to try to tempt suspicious fish into feeding.

Luncheon meat has a nasty habit of flying off the hook on the cast so you will need to take action to prevent this from happening. One method of making sure the meat stays in place is to push the hook through a cube, turn it 90 degrees and pull it back into the meat so that the point is just showing. With bigger baits it is best to introduce only a few samples as loose feed. Too many and the fish will get filled up quickly.

To give yourself the edge over other anglers, try using conventional baits in an unconventional manner. For example, mount several very small cubes of luncheon meat together on the hook. This little trick will often fool a wily old fish. The possibilities for experimentation are endless, and you should always be using your imagination to find a successful formula, one that will keep you ahead of the crowd . . . and the fish. Whatever bait you chose, whenever possible use it over a carpet of hempseed. There is no doubt that hemp is the best bait for tempting barbel into feeding.

Snaggy swims

Snaggy swims can be good spots for barbel. For instance, a sunken log can be a terrific fish-holding feature, but it can also be a real trouble spot because hooked fish head straight for cover.

If you intend to fish a snaggy swim you must use strong line, at least 8 lb. Once you strike and hit the bite, don't give the fish any line at all. It's a case of hooking and holding firm. Sometimes it may be worth walking a couple of paces in the opposite direction in a bid to stop a barbel from reaching a snag. As a precaution, pinch the barb down on your hook so that any barbel that does happen to break the line will be able to shed the hook. It is always worth trying to get them feeding away from any snag by baiting up an adjacent area.

Winter fishing

Although barbel can be caught all year round, some anglers prefer to fish for them during the colder winter months. At this time of year the most important factor is the lack of weed. Often in the summer, the angler is winding in a weed-bed rather than a fighting fish, and as a result he is having to use stronger tackle than normal to drag a fish out of weed or to prevent it getting into the weed-bed in the first place. However, winter is different because you can use tackle appropriate tor the fish itself. Furthermore, winter river fish appear fitter and fight harder, perhaps because to combat the stronger flows during this time of the year they are constantly 'working out'.

You must not fish winter rivers as though you are in a pegged-down match. It is vitally important to keep on the move, because you must search out where the fish are feeding rather than attempting to bring the few feeding fish to you.

There is no doubt that the barbel angler has to pick the right day to go fishing in winter, although certain conditions can be quite reliable. When choosing your fishing trip, always look for deep depressions in the weather pattern, especially if they are accompanied by rain, strong south-westerly winds and air temperatures rising into the upper-50°F. Do not fish within three days of a frost, and choose windy days rather than windless ones.

When it comes to the state of the river itself, barbel – and roach – do not seem to mind coloured water, whereas chub – and pike – do. Often you will find barbel and chub in the same swim. When this is the case, it is possible to entice a barbel to take your bait first. Luncheon meat is a good bait for achieving this because barbel seem to be quicker in taking it.

Although luncheon meat is probably the most successful bait for barbel, it is always worth taking a selection of others with you.

Another ploy is to feed mashed bread above the swim, and this will have the effect of dragging the chub away. You must also keep loose-feeding luncheon meat in your own swim.

Targets

What should be a realistic target for a newcomer? When setting out on this quest, any barbel, no matter what its size, is a success. Subsequently, you should adjust your target weight as and when circumstances and your experience dictate. Barbel over 8 lb are considered big, but on some stretches a barbel of such proportions is a real specimen.

Whatever size of fish you do eventually catch, do not use a keepnet to retain it. Keepsacks or tunnels are much kinder to barbel. It is worth noting, however, that National Rivers Authority rules forbid the retention of more than one fish at a time in either a sack or tunnel. Site the retainer in deep water with a steady flow and out of direct sunlight. If you have to get wet feet to reach a suitable site, you should not mind because the barbel's well-being is of paramount importance. Don't retain a barbel for longer than is absolutely necessary, especially in summer when water temperatures are high and the oxygen content low.

Above: To aid bite detection when legering, hook the line round two fingers. This will help you to feel as well as spot bites.

Left: After putting up a terrific battle, barbel need a few moments to recover. Hold the fish in the water until you feel it is ready to swim off.

65

CHAPTER SIX

TARGETING CHUB

Chub are another ideal target for the newcomer to specialist fishing because they will teach you more about the art of angling than any other species. They will melt away at the merest footfall or sudden movement, and the successful 'chub man' will be a master of concealment and stealth. Yet chub can be the most obliging of all coarse fish, and their infamous love of all things edible means they have no rival in the list of baits and tactics that will tempt them. Neither are chub shy when it comes to responding in a variety of weather and water conditions. From a blazing hot summer day to a severe winter freeze-up, chub can still be caught.

Chub are a paradoxical fish: shy and retiring if wrongly approached; greedy and voracious if a bait is presented to them naturally. They are truly a versatile quarry.

Tackle for chub

The needs of the winter chub angler are very basic. A rod, reel, landing net, some strong hooks, SSG shot, and a loaf of bread will lead to the downfall of lots of chub.

Rod choice is a personal matter, but the aspiring chub angler would be best advised to purchase a 12-ft Avon rod with a through action and a 1 lb test curve. This will enable the owner to both leger and floatfish with the same tool.

If your budget can extend to it, a second good rod choice would be a quivertip rod between 11 ft and 12 ft long with a medium action. When playing a big fish, a good chub rod will bend through to the butt, allowing the rod to act as a shock absorber to cushion the lunges of the fish. The quiver rod should take push-in tips between 1 oz and 3 oz test curve. These should be painted white for visibility and adapted to take an isotope for night fishing. Both of the above rods are ideal for small-to-medium rivers and would be unsuitable for a powerful river like the Severn or the Wye. To enable you to fish at greater distance and in the increased flow, use a powerful 1 ¼ lb specialist rod as a replacement for the Avon, and a heavy feeder-type rod for quivertipping. These are not ideal venues for the newcomer to chubbing. A small, intimate river or the upper reaches of a major river will teach you more about the habits of the chub than a spate water.

There are a number of good reels on the market, and any good, medium-sized fixed-spool will suffice, provided it can hold at least 100 m of 8 lb line. If you play your fish off the clutch, then a good clutch mechanism is essential. Carry three spools with the reel, loaded with 4 lb, 6 lb and 8 lb line, to enable a quick change to heavier or lighter tackle. Hooks should be strong. Use eyed, forged patterns in sizes 2 to 14.

The outfit is completed by a tub of SSG shot for casting weight and a round, deep-mesh, pan net. Shallow match-type pan nets are not suitable because they allow the fish to escape easily. On 90 per cent of occasions they will probably be all right, but on the occasions when you have to land a big fish in difficult swims you do not want the chub to swim out of the net.

Successful baits

If you had to carry every bait that had caught chub you would need a mobile van to transport your gear. Chub are catholic in their tastes and will take a selection of artificial, standard and natural baits. However, the choice can be simplified if you begin to consider that the selection of the hookbait should be made to give you the best presentation in any particular swim. Obviously, in coloured water, baits with a strong smell and a high density, such as lobworms, cheese and luncheon meat, are favourites. Under normal conditions, however, add bread to the list.

A fresh, uncut loaf is a superbly versatile bait, enabling you to use either flake or crust hookbaits. It is best to use crust when you want to allow the bait to 'travel' to its position in the swim. Because of its buoyancy, crust can be manoeuvred under rafts or behind weed-beds, simply by lifting the bait off the bottom. This is what is meant by choosing a bait for its ability to be presented naturally. If you believe, for instance, that the fish are at the very back of a flood raft, you will need to allow the current to work the bait into position. If you are trying to position the bait behind a rush bed on the far bank, cheese or luncheon meat would be a better choice because they will sink quickly and hold bottom rather than swing across the current.

Another point to consider is the behaviour of the bait in very cold water, cheese in particular is prone to hardening. This can be avoided if you make cheese-paste rather than

67

Above: To get the best out of chub fishing it pays to take a roving approach. It is also advisable to travel light with the minimum of tackle.

Opposite: Strike! The angler hits another chub bite and the battle commences.

using cheese straight from the packet.

Here's a typical cheese-paste recipe – equipment: cheese-grater, large round mixing bowl; ingredients: ½ lb Danish blue, ½ lb cheddar, frozen Danish/puff pastry, flavouring; method: grate the cheese and then the puff pastry into the bowl; pour in a teaspoon of flavouring; mix the flakes of pastry and cheese thoroughly together; knead the mixture into three equal balls, making sure that all the lumps are gone; place the finished balls into polythene bags and put in the freezer.

As for bait size, use a 6 hook as your guide, increasing or decreasing the bait size according to the reaction of the fish and the attention of nuisance species. Typically, pieces of crust and luncheon meat should be approximately 1 in square, and flake the size of an old 10p coin. You will catch lots of fish on unflavoured offerings, but flavourings can make a difference, particularly to bread. Cheese and meat have their own powerful, natural aroma although you can top up the cheese smell in a paste with a synthetic imitation. This is to replace the cheese smell lost by adding pastry mix to the bait. As far as bread is concerned, a white loaf can be

68

flavoured by tipping a teaspoon of carp flavour into a polythene bag and freezing it with the bread. Provided that the liquid is evenly distributed over the surface of the bag, the whole loaf will be impregnated when it thaws out by drawing the flavour in. Alternatively, for crust tear up a number of hook-size offerings and place them in a freezer bag that has a teaspoon of flavour in it, blow up the bag and give it a good shake.

Chub display a liking for lots of flavours and are particularly fond of fishy, fruity, savoury and dairy tastes.

Groundbait

Meat and cheese can be loose-fed into the swim, putting perhaps half-a-dozen samples into all the likely looking areas. However, the best groundbait of all is mashed bread. You will need stale loaves of white bread at least three days old. Stale bread can usually be bought very cheaply from a local baker.

To make mashed bread, take a large bucket and fill it one-thirds full. Break up the loaves and thoroughly soak the chunks. The soggy bread can then be 'pulped-up'. The final consistency should be such that the bread can be squeezed together with one hand. On hitting the water the bread will sink, with small fragments breaking away en route.

Alternatively, if the river is low and clear, use slightly dampened dry breadcrumbs. Using bread at least two days old, liquidise a couple of loaves until they form a loose-textured breadcrumb. Slightly dampen them in a bag, using a sponge. When you squeeze them together they should hold long enough to be fed into the swim. The effect is electrifying, with small fragments of bread cascading down from the surface for quite a distance. Dry crumb is particularly useful for fishing long glides when you wish to draw the fish to you, and it should be fed little and often.

Meanwhile, mashed bread should be fed into a swim before commencing fishing. Two or three egg-size lumps are about right as they can be topped up periodically throughout the day. If you are flavouring your hookbait you are advised to flavour the mash, adding the flavour to the water prior to adding the bread. Use one teaspoon per stale loaf used.

A good summer tactic for chub is to use Pedigree Chum Mixers, which float. Throw a handful on the water and watch them travel downstream on the current. If there are chub in the vicinity, you can be certain they will come up and take the mixers off the surface. Although chub are catholic in their tastes and will try anything, once they have been caught a few times on a specific bait they will soon get suspicious. In this respect it will again pay you to add variety by colouring and flavouring the baits. The beauty of using Chum Mixers is that some will escape downstream and be snapped up by chub in other swims. By the time you move on, the next swim is ready for fishing. In fact, you should be able to hear fish taking the bait in the distance.

In deeper swims where the river narrows and pushes the current through at a faster pace – often a haunt of big chub as well as barbel – you may need to lay a carpet of bait on the bottom to get the fish feeding. However, if you loosefeed hemp, a lot of it will be swept downstream by the current. The answer is to use a bait-dropper. This item of tackle is ideal for precision baiting, laying a carpet of bait very quickly and without disturbing the swim too much.

A bait-dropper works on a fairly simple principle. After attaching the hook to a piece of cork on the bait-dropper, the contraption is filled with hemp, the cover is replaced and the whole thing is dropped into the water at the desired spot. As it hits the river bed, a lead weight attached to a pin mechanism on the bait-dropper releases a catch and the cover opens to allow the bait to escape. Twelve droppers of hemp - about 1 pt - should be introduced in one go and then the area rested for about an hour to allow the fish to start rooting in the food on the bottom.

Bait tips

When fishing with luncheon meat, cut the meat into ½-in thick slices and tear chunks off the slice. This will arouse the chub's suspicion less than cubes of meat, and will allow small 'crumbs' to break off the main bait, thus enticing the chub from downstream. With cheese-paste, try dyeing it red with carp powder dye if you are fishing for very wary fish. To prepare breadcrust, wrap the loaf in a polythene bag and seal it, leaving it at least 24 hours before you fish. This will give you tough, rubbery crust that stays on the hook longer. For flake you will have to get a fresh loaf. Crust, however, can be refrozen and gets progressively tougher with each refreeze until it finally becomes brittle. Whatever bait you use, leave the hookpoint exposed to ensure that you hook the fish. Do not impede penetration by burying it.

Habitats

Most of our river systems contain a head of chub, although populations and average sizes vary. Canals and stillwaters, too, contain chub but location can be difficult. You will learn more about your quarry if you concentrate your initial

71

Mashed bread is a great bait for tempting river chub into feeding.

activities on small-to-medium rivers with plenty of features. You should catch fish of mixed sizes and be content to bank plenty of 2 lb and 3 lb fish with the odd larger specimen. Learn as much as you can about the habits and tastes of chub before moving on to specialise in bigger fish.

Chub are particularly fond of cover. Overhanging bushes and trees, flood rafts and undercut banks are favoured areas. Deviations in current speeds, changes in depth and weed-beds will all harbour chub. Anywhere that offers shelter and a reliable food source is worthy of investigation.

Typical chub locations on a river. Notice how these change depending on the temperatures and water levels.

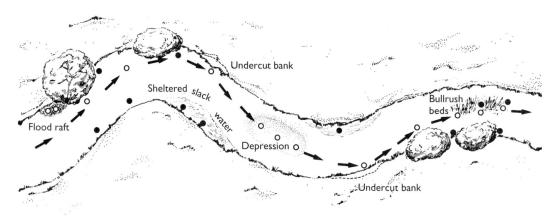

Undercut bank

Sheltered *slack water*

Flood raft

Depression

Bullrush beds

Undercut bank

○ Denotes chub spots in normal temperature/height conditions
● Denotes chub spots when low temperatures and flood spots prevail

➤ *Direction of current*

Chub are very catholic in their tastes and will even accept flavoured and coloured baits.

A particularly neglected but reliable area is the crease swim. Creases are the areas between faster and slower currents and they are excellent food carriers. Chub are fond of lying on the edge of pacier water so that they can pick off passing food items. This can be used to the angler's advantage, with bait samples introduced into the crease to draw the fish upstream. In this way large catches can be achieved by attracting fish from a considerable distance.

When fishing to features such as flood rafts, a tactical approach will score over a straightforward cast at the target. First, try to attract chub away from the cover by introducing bait samples upstream. Smaller chub will usually move upstream to intercept them and can be caught without spooking their larger brethren. Try a cast behind the feature to pick off any 'stragglers' that have followed the loose feed downstream before introducing a bait directly into the feature itself. In this way you have a greater chance of catching more than one or two fish from a good swim.

Rigs

Whereas featureless, straight areas will respond to float tactics, a roving approach using a simple leger set-up will score in most swims. The key to good chubbing is mobility and a straightforward approach to end-tackles will improve results still further.

Traditional chub leger rigs for crust have relied on very short hooklinks, but they tend to place too much weight next

73

A: This set-up has tempted many specimen chub,

B: A very simple rig to use, but still effective.

C: A good set-up for heavier flows.

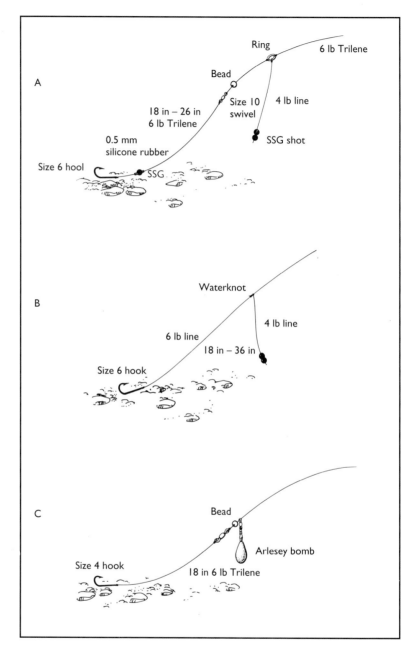

to the bait. Since you will be aiming to create minimum resistance to a taking fish, a single SSG next to the bait is all that is required. Casting weight can be applied to the link itself and this should be carefully balanced so that the rig holds bottom, but only just. Even when you are fishing a totally static bait tight to cover, the chub should feel minimum resistance and in other situations a balanced outfit will allow you to move the bait periodically, thus presenting the offering naturally without the need to recast. A search of the swim with a rolling leger is systematic and will reveal chub locations previously unsuspected. To achieve a moving bait, draw 1-2 ft of line through the rod rings, releasing it gradually so that the rig can resettle after a few feet.

When using Chum Mixers in the summer, there is no need for a float or leger weight on the line. However, it is best to treat your line with a special grease or spray, available from tackle shops, to make it float on the surface. All you need to do now is thread two Chum Mixers on a size 8 hook, cast the bait into the swim, watch it float downstream and wait for a chub to react. Once it takes the bait and you strike, the water will explode into life. As a result, it will pay you to rest the swim after you have hooked a fish.

Legering

Chub are bold-biting fish and a downstream presentation is usually adequate. However, when fishing tight to far-bank snags, an upstream leger technique gives good bite registration and allows fish to be bullied quickly out of position. Most of the time a quivertip is not a necessity, but for upstream legering it is desirable. An adequate leger weight should be used to just hold bottom, and the tip should be high in the air and carry a healthy bend. Unlike a downstream bite, which will pull the tip round, the upstream approach promotes 'drop-back' bites. Usually a small nod on the quivertip is followed by a rapid straightening as the chub picks up the bait, causing the line to go slack. Quivertips are also useful for exaggerating bites in slack or steady flows.

In the deeper swims you may experience line bites as fish competing for the loose feed bump into the line. Don't let this worry you because at least you will have proof that fish are feeding. Once you are certain that fish are present, attempt to combat the line bites by placing an SSG shot 3 ft above your leger weight. This will ensure that more line is resting on the bottom, and eliminate the problem of fish bumping into it.

The larger specimens

When it comes to size of fish everything is relative to the venue, and a specimen on any river will be a fish that is larger than the average size. On a river containing lots of 2 lb to 3 lb fish, anything above 3 ½ lb is large and a '4' is a real achievement. On a stretch containing a good head of 3 lb to 4 lb chub, a 5-pounder is a real possibility. Really big chub, fish over 6 lb, are the fish of a lifetime and they have the habit of turning up where they are least expected. Even average

75

A superb chub to brighten up even the coldest of winter's days.

chub rivers are capable of holding the odd real giant.

Catching larger-than-average fish can be simply a matter of wading through their smaller brethren, although certain short cuts can be employed. Big chub are naturally cautious and will react badly to seeing the smaller fish being caught. The hesitation of larger fish is offset by the greed of the smaller chub. They will be prepared to chase loose offerings around and can thus be drawn away from the swim, enabling the angler to present a bait to an undisturbed big fish that will have remained in position.

There can also be no question that the deeper, slower stretches of river, while containing smaller chub populations, generally hold fish of a higher average size. However, the fishing can be painfully slow and unpredictable, and you would be better advised to catch a few fish from more 'classic' stretches before tackling these canalised sections usually found immediately above weirs.

Night fishing often produces bigger than average fish and deadbaiting can be particularly productive, but make sure you can walk before you can run.

CHAPTER SEVEN

HANDLE PIKE WITH CARE

....

The modern, thinking pike angler cares for his prey. His tackle and approach reflect this attitude. He selects rigs and baits with conservation in mind and, he is aware that his behaviour in handling the fish on the bank is critical to its well being and his future sport. Such skills are not learned overnight, but are the result of long-term use of correct procedures. The condition in which a pike is returned to the water is often a measure of the ability of its captor.

The pike is an awesome-looking fish but it can provide some spectacular action.

Good handling does not start when the pike is on the bank. The use of sensible tackle and tactics in catching the fish will reduce the complications at the unhooking stage to a minimum. Tackle should be suited to the water fished. Ideally it needs to be strong enough for the job of landing pike from that water, but not so heavy that it takes away the pleasure of playing and landing them. Fishing deadbaits on a small gravel pit, for example, demands entirely different tackle to that for drifting baits across a huge reservoir. No rods and reels will be suitable for all applications. An ideal compromise that suits most piking situations is a 12 ft, 2 ¼ lb test curve carbon rod with a reel capable of holding 150 metres of 11 lb line. Pike left with broken traces in their mouths – caused by their being played on inadequate tackle – should be a thing of the past.

The end rig should be strong enough to land the pike and be simple to remove from a hooked fish. The use of quality hooks, swivels and wire is vital. Breakages can lead to rigs being left in the pike's jaw, or even worse, in its throat if poorly hooked. Barbless or semi-barbless hooks make unhooking a very simple procedure.

Bite indication must be positive. The angler must know the instant that a pike has picked up his bait. It takes only seconds for a pike to swallow a bait and become at risk of damage. Pike fishing is often a waiting game, so bite indication should preferably be both audible and visual to allow the angler time to relax and look away from his tackle for a while. Drop-off type run indicators fitted with alarms are an ideal choice.

The best run indication system in the world is a waste of time if the angler has not got the mind to strike straight away. A positive attitude is necessary. Most serious pike anglers agree that a sensible-sized bait, correctly rigged, can be struck as soon as a run is detected with near certainty that the pike will be cleanly hooked. Any delay will worsen the hooking position and increase the problem of unhooking and risk of damaging the pike.

Unhooking

A degree of firmness and confidence is required and certain items of equipment are essential. A pair of artery forceps are vital for removing hooks from the awesome jaws of the pike. Choose a size – an ideal length is 8-10 in – and style that you feel comfortable with. Some have straight ends and some are curved. Ensure that they grip well and do not spring open when you twist them. Never leave a fish unattended on the bank while you rummage through your tackle looking for them. Pike can damage themselves considerably, simply by jumping and flapping about on the bank. On occasions you may need to cut wire or a hook at the unhooking stage, so it is advisable to have a pair of wire-cutters ready just in case.

Pike should never be laid on a surface that can damage them, such as gravel banks and concrete-sided reservoirs. They are often laid on wet sacks but an unhooking mat is preferable. In a boat, line the bottom with old carpet or underlay.

Many smaller pike can be unhooked at the water's edge with a quick twist of the forceps if the hooks are exposed. Do this, if possible, to avoid handling them. Where this is not possible, place the fish on a suitable surface and apply the technique now adopted as standard by pike anglers. Kneel astride the pike – putting no weight on it, of course. Slide the first two fingers of one hand up under the gill towards the snout, taking great care not to touch the rakers, and grip the bottom jaw with these two fingers and the thumb. Slowly lift the pike's head off the ground and the jaws will open to expose the hooks. If you have used barbless or semi-barbless hooks and proper bite indication, and struck straight away, you will find the hooks easy to remove with a couple of twists of the forceps. If you have a companion, ask them to tension the trace while you are unhooking. If you are alone, grip the trace with your teeth and pull it tight. If this procedure takes more than a few seconds, you are doing something wrong and should analyse your approach to find out what.

Recording the catch

The ritual of weighing and photographing the catch is part of the modern pike-fishing scene, but it extends the handling process and can expose the fish to as much risk as unhooking does. Reduce this risk by working to a set procedure. Never hook the scales under the pike's gills to weigh it. Place it in a large sling and only lift it as far from the ground as is necessary, in case you should drop it. Do the same when you return the pike to the water. Carry it close to the ground in the sling and lower the sling into the water. Be ready for the unexpected with a big, lively pike.

Photography is simple with a friend to help you, but make sure he is getting the camera ready while you are unhooking to save time. Never put pike in keepnets, and only in a sack as a last resort. If you are alone and want a photograph, you will need to use a tripod and remote shutter release. There are endless ways of setting this up. Most anglers set up two rod-rests and frame the picture around them. Then it is simply a matter of holding the fish between the rests and treading on

79

Great care should be taken when unhooking pike. Inexperienced anglers should ask the advice of experts.

the shutter release. It takes a lot of experience to get good results, so practise with small pike until you get it right. The thing to remember is that the fish should be held safely in the sack or landing net, and only come out of the water for a very short time for the photographs. Perfect composition and exposure is wasted if the fish has split fins and scales missing. The photographs will testify to the way that you have cared for your catch.

Deadbaiting

It is a well-established fact that pike scavenge for dead or dying fish, quite readily taking them from the bottom, mid-water or even from the surface. By presenting a suitable bait, the pike angler has a very good chance of catching them. But what constitutes a suitable bait? A pike will, if hungry enough, take anything that fits into its jaws. Huge pike can swallow fish of 4 lb or 5 lb in weight, or more! On other occasions they will pick up quite tiny fish only a few inches long. The

80

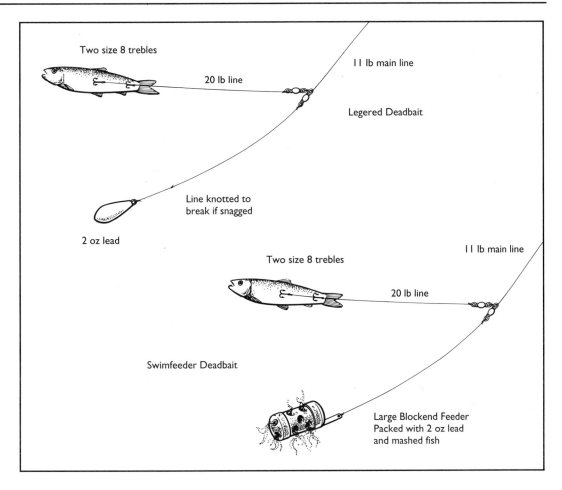

Two size 8 trebles

11 lb main line

20 lb line

Legered Deadbait

Line knotted to
break if snagged

2 oz lead

Two size 8 trebles

11 lb main line

20 lb line

Swimfeeder Deadbait

Large Blockend Feeder
Packed with 2 oz lead
and mashed fish

angler selects his bait size between these extremes and has to consider the practicalities of mounting and casting them and striking at runs, and needs to achieve a sensible compromise.

Experienced pike anglers tend to use deadbaits of approximately 4-8 in long, occasionally going slightly bigger or smaller if circumstances dictate. Such baits are easy to mount on standard rigs and will cast a good distance on suitable, balanced tackle. An immediate strike can then be applied without fear of missing a run or deep-hooking a good fish. Very hungry pike will pick up quite stale baits. Most often, though, this is not the case and they can afford to be choosy. By aiming for maximum freshness, you reduce the chances of rejection.

Deadbaits can be considered in two groups: freshwater fish and sea fish. Some waters may show a preference for one or the other, and this may need to be established with a certain amount of trial and error.

The taking of coarse fish from a water for bait may be subject to regulations and local club restrictions, and this needs to be investigated before doing so. Sometimes, such

Two rigs for a static deadbait. The diagram above is a simple legering rig while the bottom diagram shows how to use a swimfeeder for attracting pike.

81

A suspended bait. When using this rig it is possible to experiment with the depth by using a sliding stop knot. If bites are not forthcoming, alter the depth accordingly.

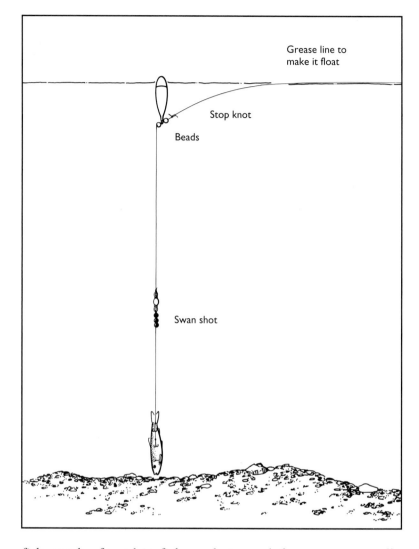

Grease line to make it float

Stop knot

Beads

Swan shot

fish can be found in fish markets, and these are generally imported from Europe. Pike will pick up any type of coarse fish. On rare occasions they might show a preference for a particularly abundant species or conversely something completely alien to the water. The more sizeable 'silver' fish are readily accepted by most pike, with roach and rudd being the most popular. For long-distance casting, slim fish like small chub and dace take some beating, whereas bream make excellent baits but do not cast well. Do not neglect perch either because, contrary to popular belief, the pike is not at all bothered by its spikey dorsal fin.

The minor species like gudgeon and ruffe work well but, by virtue of their size, generally attract a smaller class of pike. If you can get them, small pike and zander are readily taken, too. In fact, all the coarse fish species work as deadbaits. There are no hard and fast rules, so experiment!

82

Convenience, cheapness and availability have made sea-fish baits the most popular choice among pike anglers. The variety is considerable, although quality varies immensely from source to source. Freshness dictates just how long they will last on the hook, so buying them in the right condition and storing them correctly are vital considerations for economical and effective use.

Here are the more popular sea baits and their individual characteristics. The herring is an oily, clearly visible, soft fish with a strong, distinct smell. It casts extremely well when semi-frozen, but not so well when thawed out. Large herrings are just as effective when cut in half. The mackerel is another extremely popular and effective bait. It is ideal for long casting as its tough skin allows a really good hookhold when a powerful cast is used. Larger mackerel are generally used as half-baits, with the tail section being the most popular as it casts so well.

The sprat is a small, yet surprisingly effective bait, possibly due to its strong smell and very bright appearance. It is very soft fish and difficult to cast unless used with a leger rig, in which case it is best to tie the bait to the trace to prevent it from flying off on the cast. Sardines are extremely soft and need tying on for other than close-range work. They are best cast when semi-frozen, and are a very oily fish that soon become unusable due to their soft skin. Smelts, with their unique cucumber-like smell, have gained great popularity in recent years, but they need to be very fresh to retain their effectiveness and to prevent them from falling apart. Use semi-frozen for long-range casting.

A visit to a large market will often reveal all sorts of strange-looking fish on the slabs. They will all catch pike. Don't be afraid to try them if they are a suitable size, and in particular look for goat fish, snappers, whiting and scad. Small trout make excellent deadbaits, although they tend not to stay fresh for long. Their tough skin is very suitable for hooking,and they will withstand quite a powerful cast.

Finally, sections from a small eel or a whole sand-eel make ideal baits and are readily accepted by the pike. The tough skin enables a good hookhold and by virtue of this, they can be re-used several times over.

Buying and storing deadbaits

How and where you obtain your sea baits depends on how much piking you intend to do. There are three main options: pre-packed bait; fish from a stall or market; and bulk buying.

For the angler who intends to have an occasional session at short notice, the most convenient way of acquiring bait is to

83

pop into a tackle shop and purchase a couple of packs of blast-frozen, vacuum-packed baits. You can store them in your freezer at home until you need them.

More serious pike anglers make use of pre-packed baits, but will need to reduce costs if they are getting through a lot of bait. Regular trips to a fish-stall or market will eventually produce baits of the desired size and type at the right price. Snap them up while they are available and freeze them as soon as possible in readiness for the months ahead.

The ultra-keen piker, who gets through vast quantities of bait, will need to buy in bulk from a wholesaler, preferably at a fishing port where prices are lowest. This might be the only practical way of obtaining large quantities of the rarer species such as smelts. By special arrangement wholesalers will sometimes supply small fish of a suitable size, like joey mackerel, which are too small for retail sale. Delivery can sometimes be arranged, but be prepared to go and collect your bait and have a large freezer ready for it to go into. Bulk-buying with friends can make this a cheaper exercise.

When it comes to storing baits the occasional pike angler can simply pop his pre-packed baits into the ice-box of his fridge. The more serious angler with more baits to store might just get away with taking up space in the family deep-freeze. The fanatics usually have their own dedicated bait-freezer out in the garage. Small, 4-6 cu. ft, models are ideal and have sufficient capacity for a good bulk purchase. Any spare capacity should be taken up with bulky items such as bread to reduce running costs. All baits should be individually frozen, bagged and clearly labelled. The more bait you store, the more carefully you need to manage your stocks.

Static deadbaiting rigs

Armed with the knowledge required to select baits and handle pike, it is now time to move on to the exciting part – catching them! The static deadbait is a good way to start and can be rigged to catch pike in a variety of situations. You will be confronted with endless rigs for deadbaiting, but don't become confused. They are all variations on simple principles. Learn about these basic methods first, and then vary the details to suit your own particular situation.

Freelining is a commonly used method because it is so simple. All you do is tie a trace to the main line, attach a bait and you are ready to cast out. Behind the simplicity of this approach lies a great danger, however, and one that you may fail to appreciate at first. Never forget that a pike can pick up and swallow a bait in a few seconds. Any delay in indicating a run or striking a run is irresponsible and leads to deep-

hooked pike. They will be difficult to unhook and be damaged in the process. When freelining, it is possible for the pike to move a considerable distance before any run indication is given. The further the range that you have cast, the greater the possibility of this delay.

If you must use this method – and serious anglers are rapidly moving away from it – ensure that you tighten right up to the bait and set the rod on rests to show drop-back runs as well as conventional ones. If you do not do this, you will not know for quite a while that your bait has been taken. A drop-back run is indicated by the line going slack as the pike moves towards the rod. This is more difficult to achieve than one would think, and requires a bait that is quite heavy and a bottom that does not drag on the bait as you tighten up. A great degree of vigilance is required when freelining and, other than at very close range, is not recommended.

Legering is a much better way to fish if you are considering the pike's welfare. It is highly suited tor long-range work although it can be used at any range with equal effect. Use a heavy leger of about 2 oz, which will not be dragged by the pike provided the line runs freely through the lead-link swivel.

As soon as the pike moves with the bait you will get an indication at the rod-tip provided you have set the rod on rests and clipped them up tightly with no slack line. It is best

How to present a buoyant deadbait.

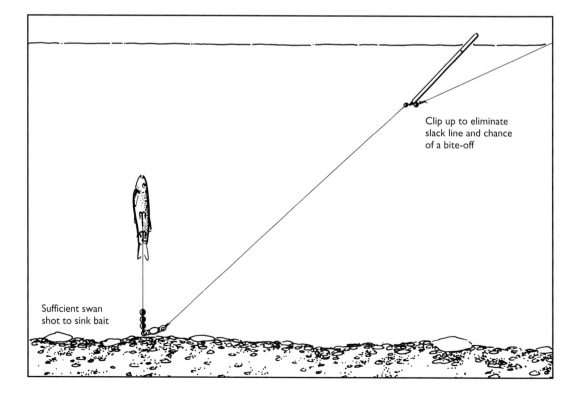

Clip up to eliminate slack line and chance of a bite-off

Sufficient swan shot to sink bait

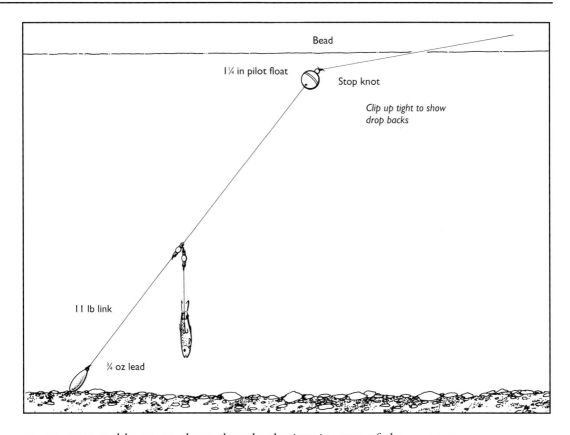

Bead

1¼ in pilot float

Stop knot

*Clip up tight to show
drop backs*

11 lb link

¾ oz lead

to set your tackle up to show drop-backs just in case of the unexpected. For example, the swivels may tangle or become clogged with weed, preventing the line from running freely. Silicone rubber tubing over the swivels reduces this problem.

A very effective way of tempting pike into feeding is to make use of a swimfeeder packed with chopped fish on the line. Put a 2 oz leger in the feeder to increase your casting range and reduce the chances of the pike dragging it, which could increase the run-indication delay time. The juices and scent given off by the chopped fish will attract pike into the swim.

A lot of anglers prefer to watch a float, and there is certainly a lot more excitement in seeing a run develop in this way than just waiting for bobbins to drop off. In theory, this approach should give the best indication of a run and enable the angler to strike right away. This is only true, however, if you are watching your floats constantly. If you cannot concentrate, use a different method. If not carried out in a responsible way, floatfishing has the same dangers as freelining – deep-hooked pike. Fish the float about one-and-a-half times the depth of the water and tighten up after casting to cock it slightly and to eliminate any slack line, hence keeping the main line away from the pike's teeth. With

Rig for a sunken float paternostered deadbait.

87

Use this rig when you need to inch-retrieve a deadbait.

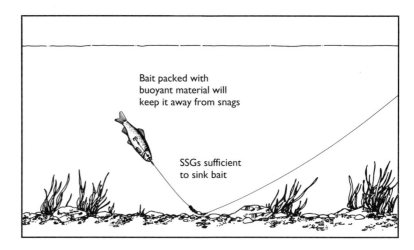

Bait packed with buoyant material will keep it away from snags

SSGs sufficient to sink bait

a non-self-cocking float, the first indication of a bite is usually the float lying flat as the pike picks up the bait. Floatfishing is most often the boat-angler's choice because rod-rests and electronic bite indicators are often difficult to set up.

On some days pike want the bait presented off the bottom. Where there are snags or dense weed, this may be the only way to proceed anyway. The easiest way of achieving this is to simply suspend a bait under a float. This has an inherent problem in that the bait will start to drift away from the desired spot if there is any breeze at all. This can, of course, be used to the angler's advantage, for covering more water, but may otherwise cause frustration. A sliding stop knot will give you the scope to change depths. Always grease the main line to prevent it sinking and becoming tangled up with the bait, leading to a bite-off.

Paternostering is the best way of suspending a bait off the bottom and preventing it from drifting away. The pike will now also have to drag the paternoster leger but unless they are particularly small pike or have been well fished for, this will not deter them at all. The length of the paternoster determines the distance from the bottom that the bait is fished. This unlikely looking method catches great numbers of pike. The float is best fished on the surface if possible, but where the bottom of the water is uneven it is often fished sunken to ensure that the main line is kept taught, reducing the possibility of tangles.

Rather than suspending a deadbait, another presentation is to bring the bait up from the bottom by making it buoyant. This is a very effective way of presenting baits over weedy bottoms and assists the pike in finding the bait more quickly. It is equally effective in open water. It can be achieved by packing the bait with a buoyant material such as balsa or polystyrene. This is not a method to be entered into lightly as there is always the possibility of a discarded bait being

88

More experienced pikers prefer to hand-line their catch into the bank. But this should only be attempted by confident anglers.

swallowed by a fish, bird or animal. To prevent this happening, tie your baits to the trace and at the end of the session account for all the pieces of buoyant material that you have used. Take them home and put them straight in the dustbin. The buoyant bait can be used in conjunction with either a leger or float. If floatfishing, ensure that the buoyant bait does not tangle with the main line by tightening up gently after casting which keeps everything in a straight line as the rig sinks.

Traces

With so many different rigs to consider, the beginner may be a little confused regarding what trace to use with each. At this stage, consider just two traces, the components of which will depend upon where you are fishing. For normal pike fishing situations, a multi-stranded wire of 20 lb breaking strain and

89

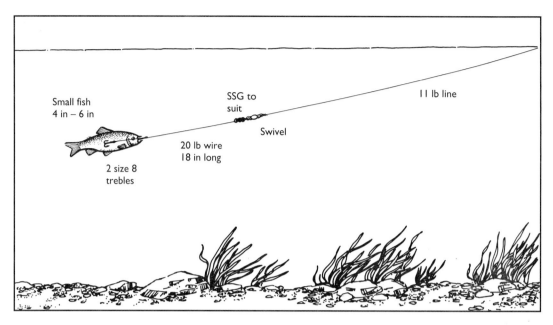

Small fish
4 in – 6 in

SSG to
suit

11 lb line

Swivel

20 lb wire
18 in long

2 size 8
trebles

A rig for a wobbled deadbait.

standard hooks and swivels will suffice. Where exceptionally large or hard-fighting fish are likely to be encountered or where conditions are rugged, when loch-fishing for example, step up to 30 lb wire and extra-strength hooks and swivels. Barbless or semi-barbless hooks are strongly recommended.

Nothing could be simpler than a one-hook rig. Take a suitable length of wire, and fix a swivel to one end and a treble to the other by crimping or twisting. Use this trace for small baits and select a hook size to suit the bait used. A size 8 covers most eventualities.

The two-hook rig is similar, but in this instance leave sufficient length of wire for tying on a second treble. The only variable to consider is the distance between the trebles. For sensible-sized baits, this should be no more than 3 in and, if anything, somewhat less. Hooks as small as a 10 might be used where runs are finicky or if there are zander about. Size 6 is suitable for larger baits or where a hard cast is required.

Moving baits

Consistent success with pike involves giving them what they want on the day. On many occasions a static deadbait fits this bill. However, there will be days when the pike will react far more positively to movement, and recognition of this fact will lead to more pike in the net. If you prefer not to livebait or if livebaiting is not allowed, you may need to put 'life' into your deadbaits to provoke a response from pike. It is often a more interesting way to fish anyway, involving the angler in much

90

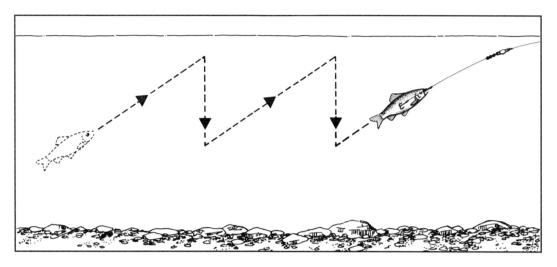

The action of a sink-and-draw deadbait.

more than just sitting and waiting. Mobile tactics have another major benefit in that they will show the bait to many more pike because they will cover a greater expanse of water.

Deadbaits cast out and retrieved in an enticing manner often spur lethargic pike into action, as well as tempting actively feeding pike. There are several ways of retrieving the bait and it is up to the angler to experiment and decide which one suits the situation in hand. The basic tackle could not be simpler, involving no more than tying a two-hook trace to the main line and adding SSG shot as necessary. It is then just a matter of casting the bait to a likely looking spot and retrieving.

The skill comes in making the fish look like a live one in distress, and also in fishing it at the correct depth and speed. Takes can come either near the bottom, in midwater or even on the surface. If the bait sinks too quickly, insert a buoyant material inside it to slow it down. Although a preference is sometimes shown for coarse fish, which look more natural than sea fish, on most occasions any small fish will suffice. Start with baits of about 4-6 in long, mounted on two size 8 trebles set 3 in apart. Vary the retrieve if takes are not forthcoming. Try a steady midwater retrieve to start with, and if this does not work, inch the bait along near the bottom, stopping occasionally. If this fails to get a take, try to make the bait rise and fall in the water to imitate a fish in trouble.

To really slow down the bait and fish more effectively over snags and weed, try suspending it under a float. This method gives the option of bringing the bait to a stop in midwater and allows time for the pike to inspect it more closely. Snatches often occur just as the retrieve is recommenced after such a stop. The take may vary from a gentle tap on the rod-tip to a violent snatch. If you are rigged correctly, an immediate strike will see the fish cleanly hooked near the front of the jaws.

91

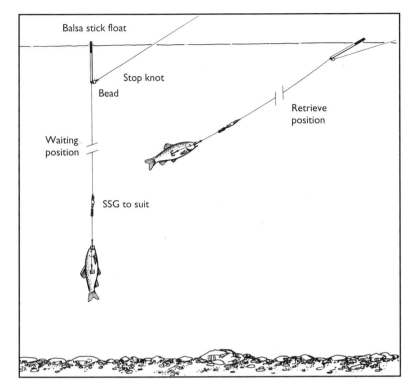

Balsa stick float

Stop knot

Bead

Retrieve position

Waiting position

SSG to suit

Opposite: Success! Pike can be safely handled by being held under the gill covers. Don't keep them out of the water for too long.

Left: A floatfished retrieved deadbait.

The mobile angler can cover a vast amount of water in a session using this technique.

On those days when nothing appears to be happening on the static baits, and you feel the pike should be feeding, try the following tactics. Go to each rod, slowly take in two or three turns of line and reset the rod on the rests. Be prepared for a snatch, as a pike will often be watching a bait, or may detect its movement from some distance away. This may be enough to induce it to take. If the water is not too weedy or snaggy you can, over a period of time, work the bait right back to the rod-tip. Even if you do not tempt a pike by moving the bait, you may move the bait closer to a pike lying inactive elsewhere in the swim. Be prepared for a take as you lift the bait from the water at the end of the retrieve. You will be amazed at the number of bonus fish this produces. Whether your bait is floatfished or legered, on or off the bottom, this technique is effective.

Just as a drifted deadbait covers a lot of water on stillwaters, so a trotted deadbait will do the same on a river, but in a much simpler manner due to help from the current. A fairly large, cigar-shaped float is ideal for this technique, and the line should be greased. If you're used to trotting a stick float or waggler down a river for species like roach and chub, you will find this method familiar. It is best carried out from a boat, so that you are not impeded by trees and bushes. By

93

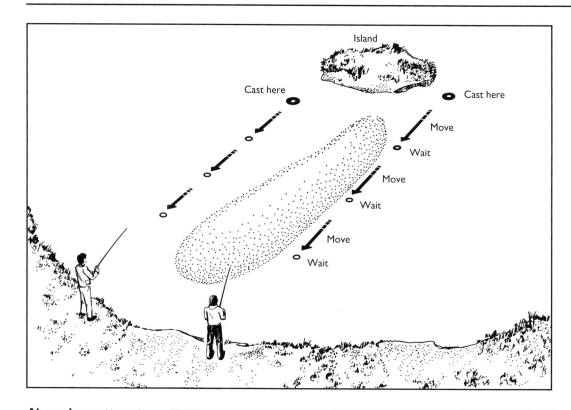

Above: In an attempt to induce a take, retrieve your baits in rotation.

Right: A trotted deadbait is effective on rivers.

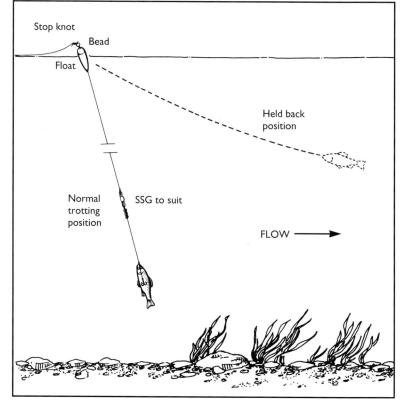

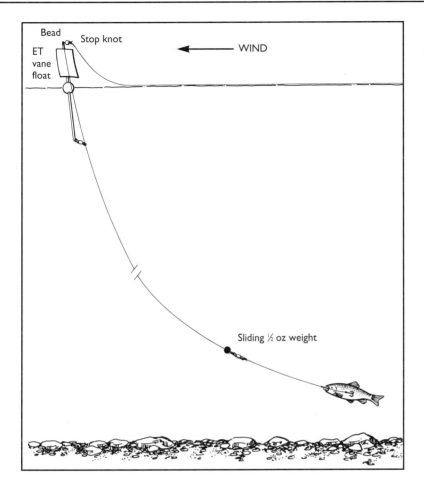

This is the set-up to use when drifting a deadbait.

anchoring in various positions, you can fish vast areas of water. Try holding the bait back occasionally by trapping the line against the reel spool. This will make the bait rise and fall enticingly in the current.

The more water a bait covers, the greater the number of pike you are likely to see. This is part of the thinking behind the drifted deadbait method. In addition, it can be used to take the bait to water beyond your normal casting range. Pike often move out of reach in this way if they are under heavy fishing pressure, or perhaps their feeding grounds are well out from the bank of a gravel pit.

Drifting may be the only way to reach pike if boats are not used on the water you are fishing. And the movement of a drifted bait may just tempt a pike not in a hunting mood to take a bait passing overhead. A major problem associated with drifting a bait lies in setting the float depth when you are fishing over an uneven bottom. The bait may, for much of the time, be fished too high in the water. When the water is particularly cold, it may not be too easy to tempt a pike to rise too far for a bait, and by employing the drifting method at

95

Trolling from a boat can be particularly effective.

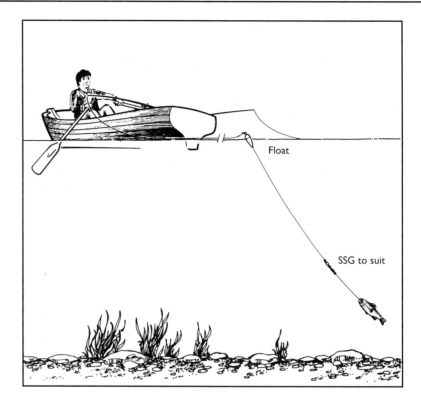

Float

SSG to suit

least you are in with a chance of some action.

As you may be drifting baits to distances in excess of 150 yd, normal striking is out of the question. It is then a matter of taking in line as fast as possible, and perhaps walking backwards at the same time. It may be several seconds before you make contact with the fish, so to avoid deep hooking don't delay. To get any speed out of the drift, and to be able to see it at a distance, a special type of float is required incorporating a large, coloured vane. Use quite a large sliding weight just above the trace to keep it upright should the weight of the bait be insufficient to sink to the bottom. Line must be well greased and it is best to use a line greaser that fits into the butt ring of the rod and greases the line as it passes through. After casting, the rod should be positioned on rests, and once the float has travelled a good distance it will start to pull line from the reel, with the bale arm open, without any assistance. A proficient pike angler could have two rigs working at the same time, but this needs extreme vigilance.

Take a pair of polaroid glasses for drifting into bright sunshine. A prerequisite for this technique is a wind of suitable strength and in the right direction. If these are not just right, all your efforts will be frustrated.

In addition to taking pike on the outward drift, never forget that the same amount of water can be covered again on a

96

slow retrieve. By walking 40 or 50 yd along the bank of a fishery, this retrieve can be made to cover previously unfished water.

A lot of specialist anglers wear camouflaged clothing on the bankside.

A boat has definite advantages. It enables you to troll or trail baits over great distances, making them available to many more pike than if you had remained static. The baits are set under floats at a depth just off bottom. In deep water, experiment with this depth as pike will often be active higher up in the water, especially during the warmer months. Grease the line and use sufficient weight to keep the bait well down in the water. Trail the baits 20 yd or so behind the boat and row along at a snail's pace. The lines are held in line clips or rubber bands on the rod butt and are pulled out in the event of a snatch from a pike. Alternatively, set rear drag or baitrunner reels to give line under the minimum pressure. As soon as the take comes, lower the anchor and strike without delay. Play the fish from the back of the boat and it should stay well clear of the anchor if you have plenty of rope out. It's an exciting method for searching vast expanses of water for pike. More specialised trolling techniques are employed for the huge deep waters, but these are beyond the scope of the beginner and should not be attempted.

97

CHAPTER EIGHT

CATCHING BIG ROACH

There's something very special about a big roach that even a tiddler-snatching matchman can appreciate. Although the roach is Britain's commonest coarse fish species, catching one of specimen proportions is still a feat to be proud of... especially in a river. A 2-pounder is usually regarded as the realisation of a river roach-angler's dream, although once that target has been achieved the enthusiast can set his sights on a fish over 3 lb.

Catching the bigger specimens takes a certain degree of knowledge and planning. You must not expect to catch large roach every time you go out, nor should you expect to catch only 'mega' roach. However good your tackle and techniques, every angler needs a bit of good, old-fashioned luck. Big fish do not like being hassled, so there is always a need to be quiet and to stay out of the fish's line of vision. However, on the positive side, big fish eat a lot, so if you get things right they are not hard to catch, as long as you do not cast on to their heads. When using the float, always start your trot well up the swim, while the bomb or feeder are both best cast beside the hotspot before being swung into place on the current.

Tackle does not need to be specialised, but well-chosen tackle can enable you to hook a few more and will certainly help to prevent lost fish. Big roach are generally bold biters, provided that they do not feel resistance too soon, so for leger and feeder work good quivertip rods are a great asset, especially if they have interchangeable tips to suit various conditions and venues. Rods should also have a forgiving action so they do not pull the hook out – a problem with big roach. When floatfishing you need a rod that will pick up a long line and set a hook, but not pull out again. For this reason it is advisable to use a waggler-style rod, even when fishing stick floats. You will spend many hours holding the rod while trotting, so investment in a first-class, light rod will make fishing easier, more efficient and more enjoyable. Reels need not be anything special. Roach, even big ones, rarely take line from you. Any landing net will do, but make sure it has a kind mesh. The same applies to keepnets, although you should not retain fish unless necessary.

Venues

Roach inhabit almost every fishery in the country. However, big roach don't. There are many venues with a reputation for specimen fish, rivers like the Hampshire Avon, Dorset and Kentish Stour, Test, Wye, Kennet and Windrush. Read the weekly angling publications because throughout the season they will carry reports of specimen roach, and the match reports may contain some good fish. Many of the top carp waters hold big roach because if the water is rich enough to produce big carp it is likely to produce big roach too. Have a walk around such lakes and pits, and ask the carp boys if they get 'bothered' by roach. If so, how big are they and where can they be found? Failing all this, you could try spending some time at your local river or lake at dawn and dusk, especially when it's fairly calm, and watch for rolling roach. Having located the fish, try to ascertain what size they are, either by observation or by catching a few. You may find a goldmine of your own.

In chalkstreams and fast-flowing rivers – the classic roach waters – during summer they prefer streamy but steady water over gravel with average depths of 4-6 ft. In cold winter conditions, they will be in an adjacent slack, and if the temperature is really low – below 40°C – it is unlikely that they will feed at all. When the temperature starts to lift and their appetite returns, try fishing the crease. If it continues to rise, roach will return to their summer position and feed in earnest. A good rule for choosing big-roach swims is to walk your stretch in summer, noting the best-looking swims – steady, streamy water with an adjacent slack – then walk the stretch again during a winter flood. Of the spots you noted in summer, even most of the slack sections will now be a boiling mess and inhospitable to fish. However, if one or two of them still look good, these are your big-roach swims, in both summer and winter. In lakes and pits fish the margins or the edge of features like bars and islands. Always be on the look out for rolling roach, and if you see some, move on to them poste-haste.

It should go without saying that the best chance of catching a big-river roach is in a river that contains a lot of them. Many anglers have not got access to the Hampshire Avon or Dorset Stour, but the chances are that your local river will still contain some big roach. Just how big depends on the water you're fishing. In some, a 1 lb roach is the maximum you

99

Above: To catch this stamp of roach you will need to choose your venue very carefully.

Right: The moment of truth as a roach is brought to the net. Is it a specimen?

100

might expect, while in others you have a realistic chance, given favourable conditions, of catching a 2-pounder. Try to set targets before fishing – a 1 lb roach might be just as much of an achievement from one venue as a 2-pounder is from another – and then spend time selecting your swim.

When selecting a swim for big roach, there are several things to remember. A swim that meets all the requirements has a better-than-average chance of producing a big roach, although a swim that boasts just a few is also worth fishing. Watch out for the following: a depth of 4-7 ft; gravel bottom in winter, between weed-beds in summer; an area of slack

When posing for the camera with your specimen fish, make sure you hold it with a firm grip.

101

water with a distinct crease between it and the main flow; beds of the weed Fontinalis, where roach spawn and usually gather as the days lengthen towards the end of the season; and rolling fish.

Don't worry if your chosen spot has relatively bare banks with no obvious fish-holding features above the water. Overhanging trees and the like have little relevance when it comes to catching roach, but they do draw in other species such as chub, which can be a nuisance when you want to catch roach. Especially in the summer, open banks can be very good, particularly if there is a shallow, gravelly area along the centre, where many roach will lie.

Timing

Both stillwater and river roach will be at their best – that is, their heaviest and most beautiful – at the back-end of the year. In rivers they recover quickly from spawning, whereas lake fish are flaccid, dull creatures at least until autumn. Weed can be a nightmare until the frosts have cleared it away, so both roach and roaching are at their best during autumn, winter and particularly towards the end of the season. Anyway, why fish for one species all year round? If you do, you are missing out on much of what this great sport has to offer.

Roach will feed throughout the day, but not as often as at dawn and dusk. As dawn gives way to day and light levels increase, big roach may become less inclined to feed. They also become easier to spook and this is probably why dawn and dusk are the best times. If you are feeder-fishing during the middle hours of the day, try to select a far-bank swim to keep disturbance to a minimum. Floatfishing at this time needs to be fine and far off.

The choice of float or leger depends as much on your personal preference as it does on conditions, except of course for really long distances when the bomb is your only option. However, one of the best methods of catching big roach must be the swimfeeder. Fish with a matched pair of bomb rods and you can try two different baits. By fishing one rod on what looks like the hotspot, and the other above, below and all around it, you will be covering all options, and if a big fish is in the area you have a good chance of catching it.

In autumn,when weeds and leaves are floating down to sea, fishing the leger or feeder is all but impossible. Fortunately, roach are particularly active at this time so the float reigns supreme. However, with the arrival of winter they are not so willing to chase a bait and will often only feed for an hour either side of darkness, so the feeder is the top method again. With an isotope on the tip of both rods you can fish into the dark – not so easy for the floatman!

Baits

Bread and sweetcorn are two baits that have caught their fair share of specimen roach. Bread is definitely the first choice for hookbait in either flake or crust form. Both of these waft around enticingly in the current, and breadflake is highly visible, especially in clear water. Crust will rise higher off the river bed – useful if the bottom contains growing weeds.

Bread can be used as a small or a large piece on the same size of hook, preferably a size 10, as long as you make sure that the hook point is showing, whatever size of bait you choose.

Bread paste is not a favoured bait for big-roach fishing. It is much more of a static bait, and if the roach are wanting a static bait, as they occasionally seem to on the hardest of days, it is better to use sweetcorn. Even when fishing with flake or crust, it is worth introducing some corn into any likely looking swims for later in the day, fed in small balls of groundbait. Although the groundbait can have the immediate effect of drawing roach into the swim, you can be certain that the corn will stay around on the bottom for longer, until you return later in the day.

It may be worth taking some red and white maggots with you, but use them only as a last resort because they tend to attract the smallest fish in a shoal.

As for feed, this too is based on bread, in three forms, liquidised, freeze-dried or mashed. Freshly liquidised slices of white bread are one of the best feeds of all for roach. If the water you intend to fish is moving slowly, leave the crusts on when you liquidise the slices so that the bread – which you squeeze into small balls and throw into the swim – sinks very slowly. For swims that are moving more swiftly, remove the crusts before liquidising and the feed will sink faster.

Unlike liquidised bread, freeze-dried bread needs water added to it before it can be thrown into a swim. It's an excellent feed with properties similar to liquidised bread. It doesn't have such a strong smell however, so it's worth enhancing it with a good sprinkling of grilled hemp. It produces a better cloud than liquidised bread, and can be good when there are'nt many roach around and you don't want to fill them up. Freeze-dried bread is available from some tackle shops, and looks like dried white breadcrumbs.

Use mashed bread for feeding prolific swims when you want some food to go down and be eaten by the roach, instead of simply forming a cloud to attract them to the area.

103

All you need for a day's river roaching – including roach.

Break a sliced loaf roughly into small pieces – crusts and all – in a bucket and wet it, mixing it well and breaking it further between your fingers until it can be squeezed into a loose ball and thrown, and sinks once in the water.

Targets

A realistic target depends very much on where you live. On the Hampshire Avon you need to hit that magic 2 lb mark to be satisfied, while on other rivers and lakes a fish over 1 1/2 lb would be splendid. Before you start to travel miles to fish a top water, get as much experience as you can on local venues. Your local 1-pounders could be harder to catch than 2-pounders from the Hampshire Avon. So practise your methods and skills on these type of venues and you will be in good shape to tackle those dream-roach rivers as soon as you get to them.

104

CHAPTER NINE

OTHER SPECIES

PERCH

In recent seasons there has been evidence of an increase in the level of perch activity, with anglers experiencing good sport on British rivers, canals, drains and lakes. More and more people are fishing solely for this species as it makes a welcome return to prominence. Gone are the bad days of the 1960s and 70s when the perch population suffered from a disease called aeromonas bacteria, which caused ulcers on the sides of their bodies. Stocks were decimated by the disease, and in some parts of the country they still have not fully recovered. It was, perhaps, nature's way of redressing

The distinctive appearance of a perch, including spikey dorsel fin.

These two rigs are ideal for laying a bait on the bottom.

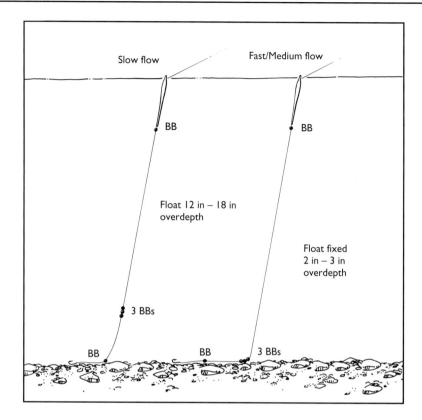

Slow flow

Fast/Medium flow

BB

BB

Float 12 in – 18 in overdepth

Float fixed 2 in – 3 in overdepth

3 BBs

BB

BB

3 BBs

the balance because, left unchecked, perch can quickly over-run a fishery. The few survivors that were left behind grew into large specimens as the competition for food decreased. Many venues are now producing extremely good catches of fish, and the perch is certainly becoming a big-fish angler's target again.

Lakes

The perch is probably the first fish an angler will catch, but it will be more by luck than judgement. So how do you set about catching them on purpose? Perch can be found in virtually every type of fishery from lakes to rivers. During a pleasure-fishing session or even in match surroundings an angler, through regular and accurate feeding, will most probably attract a perch or two into the swim. Few anglers, however, set out with the intention of fishing solely for perch. Yet this species can provide a superb day's fishing for those willing to spend time searching for a shoal.

One of the best fisheries in which to try to catch big perch is a gravel pit. Even if the fishery is several acres in size, swims should be approached with care. Perch are like chub because they will accept fairly crude tackle, but will be

106

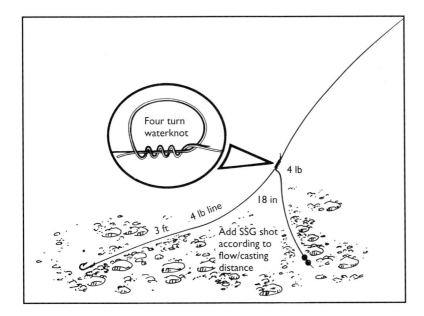

A simple link-leger rig.

Four turn
waterknot

4 lb

4 lb line

18 in

3 ft

Add SSG shot
according to
flow/casting
distance

spooked by any commotion on the bank. In waters like gravel pits you will have to use fairly heavy gear because many contain pike as well, and often a pike will take a bait intended for a perch. A bright and sunny day and fairly clear water are always the ideal conditions for perch because they are sight hunters.

It pays to experiment with different techniques, especially on a big expanse of water. If there is a favourable wind blowing, a good method to try is a drifted fish bait because it is ideal for covering a wide area. The idea is to suspend a bait below a round pilot float, which is allowed to drift in the wind.

If the gravel pit is weedy you may have to drift the fish bait above the weed, which can be very dense in places, growing anything from 12 in to 3 ft off the bottom. The perch tend to hide themselves in clear patches. Often as the bait drifts over these holes in the weed-bed the perch will be tempted from their homes and snatch at the bait. It is important to grease your line to make it float because this helps the tackle to drift along with the surface skim.

As an alternative to a drifted floatfished bait, try a wobbled deadbait using the same tackle. All you need to do is remove the pilot float and re-tie the main line to a link swivel and wire trace. After lip-hooking another fresh bait, cast out and allow the bait to sink slightly before the retrieve. Perch prefer a steady retrieve, whereas pike seem to like an erratic one. As you wind in line slowly, the bait will wobble enticingly through the water. Hold the rod at a 45-degree angle to the line and if you feel a fish taking the bait, point the rod-tip straight at the fish. You give the perch a bit of slack line in this

107

way, it should not feel any resistance and there is less chance of it ejecting the bait. Then it is a case of counting to four and striking by winding the reel as fast as you can. There is no need for a vicious strike.

Another good, searching method for perch is lure fishing. The beauty of these first three ways of catching perch is that you will not have to change tackle for any of them. For lure fishing simply put on a new wire trace with a clip link, which is then connected to a lure. A lot of nonsense is talked about lures and they probably catch more anglers than fish. If a perch or pike isn't interested in one particular lure, it will probably ignore others cast to it as well. So don't buy lots of lures. At first, stick to the popular designs and as you become more proficient begin to experiment with other patterns.

Rivers

One of the beauties of fishing for perch in rivers is that you do not have to spend much on baits because one of the most successful is worms. All you need to do on the eve of your

109

fishing trip is to collect a bait-box full of lobworms off your garden lawn. If the grass is damp after rain or heavy dew, the task of collecting lobworms is easy because a lot of them will be lying with most of their bodies outside their holes in the ground. However, a worm will quickly disappear if it senses you approaching, so tread carefully. The secret is to trap the worm with a finger and then gently ease it out of its hole with your other hand. Overnight, store the worms in a mixture of grass, moss and damp, torn-up newspaper. If you intend to keep them for a longer period, put them in a bucket and throw a few potato peelings in for the worms to feed on. To make your bait last longer it is best to use half a worm on the hook while loose-feeding maggots.

When it comes to swim choice on a river, look for any spot with cover. It could be an overhanging tree, old cabbage beds, reeds, undercut banks or lay-bys off the main course of the river. Any swim that has a combination of all or a few of these should turn out to be a real hotspot. Deep, slow stretches, commonly found above weirs, hold a lot of perch in winter, while in summer and autumn you need to find areas where the flow is slightly stronger than the norm. During this time look for the outside of bends, where the river narrows and the water speed increases, or the final 100 yd above a weir as the water drives off.

The best method for locating perch is legering. You can fish for bites on the leger, and once they start coming you can change to floatfishing tackle. However, if you are forced to fish in faster flows, legering should become your number one choice throughout the season. Keep your leger rig simple because all you need is enough weight to cast out and hold bottom. Pinch two SSG shot on to an 18-in link of 4 lb line, and with this simple method you can either add or take off shot according to the flow or casting distance.

When floatfishing, it is best to use a stick float carring about 4BB. The float should be shotted with a BB underneath the float to act as a depth marker, 2BB placed together at half-depth and two No. 4 spaced out below. After autumn, when the leaves have fallen off the trees and are starting to sour the river-bed, it is advisable to fish a bait a few inches off the bottom. Perch are reluctant to grub around and they much prefer a clean bait suspended just above the decaying leaves. It is best to let a bite develop because often a fish will cause a series of dips on the float-tip before taking it confidently. If you strike too soon, it is more than likely that you will pull the worm-baited hook out of the perch's mouth. Another floatfishing method worth trying when things get hard is laying the bait hard on the bottom. You can fish a float 12-18 in overdepth with a bulk of 3BB 18 in off the bottom and a further BB on the bottom. This is a particularly good rig for fishing a float next to overhanging trees and underwater cabbages in slow flows. In swims where the water is a little pacier, fix the float 2-3 ft overdepth with the bulk shot resting on the river bed.

BREAM

If you consider anything over about 8 lb as being a big bream there are plenty of waters of all categories capable of producing numbers of such specimens. These days, however, most specialists would be looking for fish into double figures, and for bream of this calibre large stillwaters offer the best prospects. When you start looking at fish in excess of 12 lb,you will have to concentrate your efforts on three types of water: certain reservoirs, gravel pits, and some of the Shropshire and Cheshire meres. The vast majority of huge bream caught in recent years have come from waters in these categories.

However, it is better to walk before you can run. Assuming you have taken bream to, say, 3 lb or 4 lb and now wish to progress to something better, the greatest mistake is to switch to an ultra-slow gravel pit in search of a double-figure fish. Of all specimen hunting, fishing for bream can be the most heartbreaking and unrewarding in terms of fish landed. The best advice is to concentrate your efforts on a water with a large head of bream up to, perhaps, 8 lb in weight. It is vitally important to have a lot of average-to-good fish under your belt before graduating to the real heavyweights. Some of the Midlands reservoirs and estate lakes contain large shoals of bream that are not too difficult to catch, and it is these fish that the inexperienced specimen hunter would be wise to cut his teeth on.

Once you have chosen your water, the next consideration must be locating the shoals of bream. Many reservoirs are fairly featureless bowls, and swims in this type of water, rather than existing naturally, can often be created by baiting-up. Gravel pits, by their nature, are usually full of features such as gullies, drop-offs and gravel bars, and the latter is a known feeding ground for big bream. The best way of locating such features is undoubtedly by use of a boat and echo-sounder. If you do not possess an echo-sounder, a long, extendable pole used from a boat will find the features, but it is a much slower process. To find features from the bank, use a large sliding float coupled with a heavy leger weight that sinks the float. Set the float shallow at first, cast to maximum range and then retrieve a few feet at a time, making sure to let out slack line after each retrieve.

If the float pops up at any point you have found an area

111

Bream are not the most hard-fighting of fish but specimens will put up a dogged battle.

shallower than the float setting. By doing this at several depth settings and from different swims, you soon get an idea of the main features in front of you. Another tip is to locate areas that are naturally free of heavy bottom-weed. There is now evidence to suggest that bream do not like to feed in heavy weed, and even swim clearance produces poor results. Fish spotting is a proven technique on Cheshire meres, but finding swims in this manner on large gravel pits is a non-starter. To see a rolling bream is rare, but if one is spotted it is a bonus, so take full advantage of it.

Prebaiting is important because if a shoal of big bream do move in, they will clear all available food very quickly. You need to hold the fish long enough to have a chance of catching one or two. The best kind of prebaiting is one that encourages the bream to stay in the swim to search out small, individual food items or particles. This is much more effective than just using cereal feed, especially on hard bottoms. The best particles to use include casters, squatts, corn, boiled rice and stewed wheat. In very soft-bottomed waters, where heavy particles such as wheat can disappear into the silt, mashed bread with light particles of fluffy rice or casters

would be a good choice.

If you had to choose one hookbait for bream, it should be a full-sized lobworm. However, specimens have been caught on maggots, casters, redworms, sweetcorn and breadflake. Modern carp baits, fished both as pastes and boilies, have also taken a few fish, and it is possible that an extensive boilie campaign would wean them on to the bait. Cocktail baits are also worth a try, and many good fish have been caught on lobworm/corn, lobworm/paste, lobworm/flake, corn/maggot, corn/caster and maggot/flake.

The best method for big bream is determined by practicality as much as anything else. Big bream rarely come close into the margins, and the majority of swims are at fairly long range. That, plus the undeniable fact that specimen

The roving angler can have great fun with zander. Lure fishing is a great method for locating shoals of fish.

113

bream are largely nocturnal in their feeding behaviour, means that legering is the only viable approach on most waters. The exception would be where you are allowed to fish from a boat, in which case laying-on with a betalight float at night could be a deadly method, but you must consider the safety factor. Most top bream anglers would advocate the use of a fixed paternoster rig with a short, heavy leger link and a longer hooklink – the set-up that is known as the helicopter rig in carp-fishing circles.

The tackle for bream fishing needs to be specialised only to overcome the physical problems encountered, not to deal with the strength of the bream themselves. As many swims are at long-range, the rods need to be capable of handling the long casting involved. Similarly, as heavy terminal tackle will be required to give casting weight, it is folly to attempt to fish with too light a line or you risk breaking off on the cast. For the long hours of waiting involved in big-bream fishing, much of it at night, audible alarms such as optonics are an absolute must. Use 8 lb main line and braided hooklinks of 6 lb, and hook sizes will depend on the bait being used. For a large bait such as a lobworm use a size 6 hook, while for maggots and casters a size 12 is adequate.

It has to be said that when an angler is obsessed with specimen bream, it is not because of their spectacular fighting ability. Generally, big bream put up a mediocre struggle. Where they are found in rivers they often give a fair account of themselves, using their broad flanks to full advantage in the current. Although stillwater bream are usually lethargic fighters, even very big ones, there are the occasional exceptions, particularly if you hook a male in early season. The danger with playing bream comes from their large body area, and if one is swimming side-on to you it will create enormous resistance when you try to turn it, and this can lead to hooks being pulled out. The deep body of the fish also makes them very difficult to bully free if they become weeded. For this reason it is best to hold a hooked bream hard in the initial stages of the fight, to bring it up in the water out of harm's way.

ZANDER

Zander are not often widespread in a water because they tend to hunt in groups or packs, and large areas may be devoid of them. When not active, they will often congregate in large numbers. Drop on them and it could be all action. It is often an 'all-or-nothing' exercise, but get it right and you could be in for a big haul.

The secret of success is to search as much water as possible until contact is made. If you stay in one swim, there is always a chance that a feeding pack may pass through because on occasions they will hunt over a wide area. A far better approach is to keep on the move until you find them or your paths cross.

Experienced zander anglers are well aware of situations that improve their chances of a successful session. In coloured water, for instance, zander feed more confidently. Areas that are constantly coloured are often colonised by zander provided there is a plentiful supply of small fish for them to eat. Colour caused by an influx of floodwater often induces a change in their feeding pattern. If they have been night feeding, as they often do when the water is very clear, they will suddenly become active during the daytime as the water becomes really murky. A reasonably heavy flow on a drain or river does not bother them unduly, but run detection may be difficult at such times due to floating debris.

Zander eat fish, it is as simple as that. It is more important to find good concentrations of small fish than to seek out nice-looking swims and features. Some of the best zander swims look totally barren. Under the surface it may be a different matter, though. On many waters, small fish may only be seen dimpling at dawn and dusk. Be there at the right time, otherwise you might miss them and also the accompanying zander.

A method called leapfrogging has become a standard searching approach for zander specialists on the Fenland drains and rivers. Start on a stretch of water that you feel has zander potential. Spend half-an-hour in a swim and if no runs are forthcoming, start moving your rods along the bank to the next swim by transferring the end rod to the forward position. This approach is best carried out with several friends, because a lot of water can be quickly explored. If a zander is caught or a run missed, spend a little longer in that area. You might contact a pack of zander on the move and, if you are floatfishing, your runs will sometimes indicate which way they are travelling. You can then try to follow them.

Good areas to try are sidestreams and outfalls. Water pumped or flowing into a river or drain from a sidestream or small drain will bring with it all sorts of food to attract small fish into the vicinity. These spots are best tried after a period of regular, heavy flow and especially if the water colours up. However, any feature that will attract small fish, be it for food or cover, will be worth trying. Look for fallen branches and extensive reed-beds and cabbage patches, and especially where these features are not widespread on the water.

When searching the Fenland drains and rivers, get to know the bottom contours. The vagaries of dredging may see depth variations here and there which, in an otherwise barren piece

115

Zander were once regarded as villains, decimating fish stocks. But now they are regarded as a legitimate target for specimen hunters.

of water, may be the only feature of any note. In particular, one side of the drain may be considerably deeper than the other if the water has been dredged from one bank only.

When winters are mild, zander become a worthwhile proposition throughout the whole of the season. Only prolonged cold weather will slow their feeding down. However, zander are known for their unpredictability, and even if a swim contains them you still might not catch a fish. For reasons best known to themselves, they may be predominantly night feeding and you will waste your time fishing the daylight hours. Where they have ample food supplies, they will feed in short bursts and then be inactive for long periods.

116

SPECIALIST ANSWERS

By now you must be ready to go out on the river bank and catch that fish of a lifetime. However, you must be patient because 2 lb roach and 5 lb chub are not easy fish to catch. Follow the advice in this book and make sure you prepare thoroughly before embarking on a big-fish campaign. Set yourself realistic targets at first, and you will enjoy moving up the scale towards specimen catches. Don't go out and buy all the fancy gear straight away because you may find that you would rather go stalking for chub in a river than sitting behind a pair of matching rods, waiting for a massive carp to take your bait. However, once you have experienced the thrill of landing a specimen fish, you are sure to want to extend your scope.

In this final chapter, experienced specimen hunters answer some of the questions often asked by those new to this branch of the sport.

Q *I want to fish a venue where I know there are big carp, but every time I visit it the water is always cloudy. How do I find the hotspots?*

A You must look for other signs like rolling fish, bubbles, boils and reed movement. If it's a water that contains only carp, you will quickly be able to build up a picture of the prime feeding spots. Don't fish 'blind' because you could waste hours, even days, if it is a big fishery. If in doubt, ask an angler who fishes the venue regularly, and he will probably be only too pleased to offer some advice. Do not expect him to give too much away, but a little guidance will go a long way.

Q *When plumbing the depth with a leger, how do you know the depth of a swim?*

A You can only really estimate the depth with a leger. Plumb a swim with a float first to find the exact depth, and then cast a leger to it and count how long it takes for the weight to reach the bottom. Divide this number into the depth you have discovered with the float, to get a feet per second figure. This can now be your guide for finding the contours of the swim, especially for those distances out of range of the float. Do not be too worried about the exact depth. It is more important to discover the bottom contours of a lake – the drop-off points and shelves. Using a leger in this way is a good aid to swim selection.

Q *I have heard that a lot of tench anglers use the 'lift' method. Could you explain what this is?*

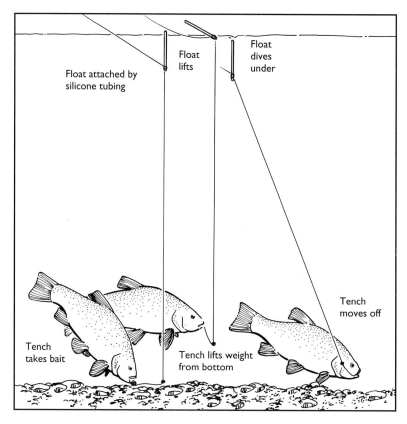

Float attached by silicone tubing

Float lifts

Float dives under

Tench takes bait

Tench lifts weight from bottom

Tench moves off

A The 'lift' method is a good early-season floatfishing tactic for tench. The float is set overdepth and the bait is anchored to the bottom by an SSG shot placed close to the hook. A bite is often indicated by the float lifting and lying flat on the surface.

Q *If I find the features of a lake at one time of the year – say the close season – will my picture of the venue change with the seasons?*

A The features of the lake will not actually change very much except maybe for silt deposits, which will get deeper as the years pass. Although you may have built up a fairly good picture during your exploratory plumbing and feature-finding sessions, it is still worthwhile re-checking a few areas from time to time because although the depth of the water will not vary very much, except in times of drought, the 'feel' will because the fish will be constantly changing their feeding spots. Therefore, if you find an area that feels like clean gravel, that you didn't find on previous visits, there is a good chance that fish are present. They have probably recently used this area to feed on and cleaned the gravel in the process. Location of these spots can be vital because they are sometimes very small, and a bait presented near to but not on the area could be completely ignored, whereas a bait presented 'on the money' will be productive. If you can imagine it, it is rather like being blindfolded and then trying to cast your line around your dining-room on to the dinner plate.

Weed growth, if there is any present, will vary throughout the season and from season to season, and as fishing in and around weed-beds can be productive this will have to be taken into consideration as and when the situation arises. Knowledge the contours of a lake will help you to ascertain where you should present your bait in relation to weed-beds. This knowledge will be invaluable season after season in spite of other changing characteristics.

Q *Even if I keep an underwater map of a lake in my notebook, how can I be sure I'm casting into the right place on my next visit to the water?*

A The only way to ensure you are casting to the right place on your next visit is to memorise the contours in conjunction with the far bank. For example, if you find a gravel bar at roughly 70 yd range in line with a particular tree, bush or some other object on the far bank, jot this down in your notebook. It may even be worth taking a few photographs of the lake and taking these with you on your feature-finding visits. Mark the float's position on the photographs as and when you find the features. The more information you put down in your notebook the better, and it is then a case of memory and experience. The more experience you have and the more you can memorise a situation, the better angler you will become. Obviously, on your fishing visits you can quickly re-check the features of your swim if you already have a good idea of the area from looking in your notebook. It is then a case of leaving your marker float in the position that you wish to fish.

119

This angler managed to tempt the largest fish of the shoal.

Q *Is there any way of making sure I catch the largest fish in a shoal of chub I can see in the water?*

A This is very difficult. The largest chub tend to be the craftiest of all and the most wary of people. However, some specialists have developed a method whereby they feed a spot and watch the fish for perhaps several hours. Usually the smallest, most greedy chub gobble up the mashed bread first, but eventually the biggest move in and drive the smaller ones away. That is the signal to drop a bait among them.

Once you have caught a fish from a shallow river, it can be difficult to tempt another straight away. The commotion caused by your first fish as you play it is likely to frighten others off. However, if it is a good swim and a natural holding spot where the fish like to live, it is certainly worth another visit later in the day.

120

Q *I like to fish in all weathers, but struggle when it is really cold. Could you give me any tips?*

A First, wrap up warm or you will soon be heading for the comfort of your home, and it is best to keep on the move, especially if you are not catching in a particular swim. For the best results, try the hours of darkness because very often fish will feed at night even as the temperatures plummet. Millponds are good fish-holding areas in rivers in winter, and they usually do not freeze up as quickly as the main river. Carry a pair of polarising glasses with you. During the winter months the sun is usually low in the sky, causing a nasty glare off the water's surface. To avoid your rod rings from freezing up, treat them with a substance like vaseline. On really cold days ice may still form in the rings, but the addition of vaseline will help. Finally, don't make a commotion on the bank because stealth will always pay dividends.

On those cold winter days make sure you wrap up warm.

121

Q *I keep getting small twitches on my lobworm bait, but cannot connect with any chub. Am I doing something wrong?*

A Probably not. The chances are that the culprits are not big chub at all, but smaller fish like dace and roach plucking at the tail of the lobworm. If these fish are in your swim, your best bet would be to change baits to something like a large piece of breadcrust or flake. These nuisance fish will probably ignore it, but the big chub won't. Alternatively, you could wait until the tip really pulls sharply round to signal the arrival of a chub.

Q *When using boilies for tench, do you need to fish the bait on a hair rig?*

A At first try to fish a boilie on the hook itself. If you feel the tench are getting suspicious of the bait you can change to a hair rig. This hair rig should be an extension of your hooklink after it has been tied to the hook. All you need to do is leave a short piece of nylon that can be formed into a loop. A single or double boilie could then be threaded on to the loop and fixed with a boilie stop.

Q *Apart from lakes, what other venues hold good heads of tench?*

A Tench also love drains and canals, and most rivers contain a quantity of the species. As a general rule, if you find a cover of lily-pads or reeds, tench will not be too far away. In fact, tench can tolerate low oxygen levels and therefore survive in tiny, overgrown waters. As long as they can search among the roots of water plants for food like snails, and bloodworm in silty water, tench will flourish.

Q *How do you prevent a big fish from getting into a snag?*

A If you intend to fish a snaggy swim you must use strong line. Once you strike and hit the bite do not give the fish any line at all. It is a case of hooking and holding firm. Sometimes it may pay you to walk a couple of paces in the opposite direction to the fish in a bid to stop it reaching a snag. As a precaution, pinch the barb down on your hook so that any fish that does happen to break the line will be able to shed the hook easily. It is always worth trying to get fish feeding away from any snag by baiting up an adjacent area.

122

Q *What is it about peanuts and tiger nuts that injures and sometimes kills carp?*

A Many angling clubs have imposed bans on particle-type baits because in a few isolated cases fish have died due to eating bait that was badly prepared by anglers. It is vitally important to take the utmost care when preparing particles. All nuts, beans, peas and seeds – unless they have come out of a tin – should be soaked in water for at least 24 hours before they are used or, in the case of those that need it, placed in boiling water. The reason for this soaking is because most nuts, beans and peas will absorb water and then swell up. Obviously, a fish with a gut full of unswollen beans will have a digestion problem, which in some cases could prove fatal. The right preparation must be undertaken before you fish with nuts.

Q *How can you fish exclusively for perch? Won't lobworms attract other species?*

A Location is the key to success with perch. Once you have found a shoal you will be able to catch perch after perch on lobworms. Watch out for the features mentioned in Chapter Nine as more often than not they will hold perch. Speak to other anglers, including matchmen, who should be willing to tell you where they have caught numbers of perch. Obviously, other species like roach and chub will pick up a lobworm intended for perch, especially in winter as the fish move into deeper water.

Q *When is the best time of year to fish for zander?*

A Zander do not seem to be caught during extreme temperatures; for instances, when it is very warm or bitterly cold. Usually, mid-September until the first frosts finds them feeding well at some time of the day or night. At other times sport can be very patchy. Round-the-clock fishing over a period of time is the only way to establish their preference, and this may well change as conditions alter. Once this is established, local anglers can take advantage of short sessions at the optimum time. This is often the reason why travelling anglers, not in touch with the water, struggle to catch them.

Q *I have prebaited a swim. How can I make sure I fish it on the opening day of the season?*

A If you have prebaited a swim, there is absolutely no guarantee you will get to fish it on the first night or opening day. It is probably best to tell other anglers which swim you

123

have prebaited in the hope they will leave it for you. If they don't, they are not very nice people. Don't despair though, as it is just the start of the season. You will have nine months to go, so you will probably win in the end.

Q *On the water I fish regularly, the best catches seem to be taken at night, but I'm frightened of the dark. What should I do?*

A If you are frightened of the dark do not even consider night fishing. There can be many weird sensations for people unused to being alone at night. Some anglers love the atmosphere, others hate it. The best advice is to improve your technique as these big fish will feed at some point during the day. Using watercraft and skill, there is no reason why you should not hook a biggie in the daylight hours. However, if you fish a lake regularly there must be one or two anglers who go night fishing. Speak to them and explain your fears. Eventually, you will find someone who will be willing to invite you on an overnight session. After a couple of sessions accompanied by another angler, you will be ready to go it alone. Enjoy it.

Don't go night fishing if you are afraid of the dark.

Q *I fish a very popular barbel river and have been frustrated by missing a number of false bites. Is there a remedy for this problem?*

An angler admires his barbel catch after correctly spotting a true bite.

A The vast majority of tentative indications when fishing for barbel with a particle bait/swimfeeder combination are line bites. Unless you want to alarm the fish in the process, ignore anything other than deliberate pulls. Proper bites are instantly recognisable for what they are, by the rod-tip being pulled right round and staying there. When floatfishing with hempseed as bait, slip a length of snug-fitting silicone tubing over the shot. This deters fish from taking the shot in mistake for hempseed. The tubing also helps to cut down the risk of tangles.

Q *I have great difficulty in keeping luncheon meat on the hook. I either lose it on casting, or the fish snaps it off the hook without hooking itself. How can I rectify this problem?*

A Luncheon meat can be encouraged to stay put by various means, and it is easier to keep several small pieces in position rather than one big chunk, particularly in hot weather. One

125

method entails sliding a plastic tube on to the hooklink directly above the hook. After baiting the hook, push the tube into the meat - this prevents the line from cutting through the meat when you cast. A small pad of something soft, such as a pinch of bread, on the bend of the hook also helps. A favourite method is a variation of the hair rig and entails tying a small-diameter stiff piece of plastic in the middle of the hair, so that a T-shape is formed. The plastic must be long enough to pass through the bait. Align the plastic and hair, push them through the meat, release the plastic and slide the bait down the hair. The plastic now forms a T-shape with the hair again, thus preventing the meat from flying off. Failing these ploys, switch to a slightly different bait that stays on better.

Q *As a beginner to carp fishing, should I concentrate on easier venues at first?*

A If you are a beginner to carp fishing, it is preferable to concentrate on easy venues where you can gain experience of baits, rigs, tackle, location and handling fish. Once you have gained sufficient experience in all of these, you can then move on to other waters and the challenge of catching bigger fish. If you begin on a hard water you will find the learning process extremely slow and will probably get bored with carp fishing. It is generally best to stick to one or two venues in the early stages because you will learn a lot more about them. If you continually skip from one venue to another, you will not learn anything about any of them. At the end of the season it might be a case of fishing everywhere, but catching very little.

INDEX

Other Fishing Titles Available from Boxtree:

1-85283-181-2	Wilson's Angle	£9.99
1-85283-182-0	Go Fishing Year	£10.99
1-85283-156-1	Go Fishing	£9.99

Improve Your Coarse Fishing Series:

1-85283-190-1	Float Fishing	£9.99
1-85283-187-1	Pole Fishing	£9.99
1-85283-188-X	Legering	£12.99
1-85283-189-8	Baits	£12.99
1-85283-443-9	Match Fishing	£12.99

Angling Times Library:

1-85283-122-7	1: Carp	£9.99
1-85283-123-5	2: Tench	£9.99
1-85283-124-3	3: Chub	£9.99
1-85283-126-X	4: Pike	£9.99
1-85283-152-9	5: Bream	£12.99
1-85283-153-7	6: Barbel	£12.99
1-85283-151-0	7: Roach, Rudd & Dace	£12.99

All these books are available at your local bookshop or newsagent, or can be ordered direct from Littlehampton Book Services, tel: 0903 726 410.

Prices and availability subject to change without notice.

YOU'VE READ THE BOOK NOW READ THE MAGAZINE!

Improve Your Coarse Fishing magazine is Britain's best selling fishing monthly and is always full of great articles, tackle reviews and hundreds of hints and tips from all the best anglers to help you catch more fish and enjoy your sport.

If you want to improve your angling technique then this is the magazine for you.

Improve Your Coarse Fishing is on sale from the 19th of every month.